THE ULTIMATE LIFE SKILL

How to Break Free from Our
Performance and Perfection Obsessed
Culture and Be More Fulfilled

DR. PETER KRISTIANSEN

Capucia LLC
211 Pauline Drive #513
York, PA 17402
www.capuciapublishing.com
Send questions to: support@capuciapublishing.com

Paperback ISBN: 979-8-9915156-3-4
eBook ISBN: 979-8-9915156-6-5
Library of Congress Control Number: 2024923684

Cover Design and Layout: Jeevan Panesar
Editor: Karen Burton

Printed in the United States of America

Capucia LLC is proud to be a part of the Tree Neutral® program. Tree Neutral offsets the number of trees consumed in the production and printing of this book by taking proactive steps such as planting trees in direct proportion to the number of trees used to print books. To learn more about Tree Neutral, please visit treeneutral.com.

Disclaimer

The story, all names, and characters portrayed in this production are fictitious. No identification with actual persons (living or deceased), places, buildings, and products is intended or should be inferred.

CONTENTS

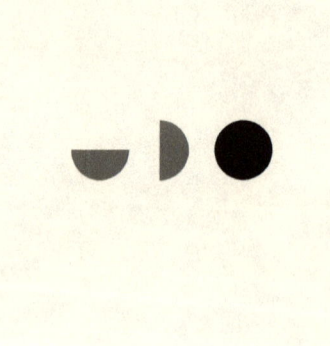

INTRODUCTION

This Book Has the Power to Change Your Life Forever

If you've read any of the books on the self-help shelves or have taken one or more self-help seminars that promise happiness—but have not found the long-term benefits you're looking for in your life—the information in this book might be exactly what you need. If you don't want to buy into the spiritual or metaphysical ideas that are so prevailing in the self-help arena today—but instead want knowledge based on common sense and science—let's get started.

Deep inside, we all want to feel good about ourselves and the life we live, and we yearn to feel fulfilled. In order to experience that, we need to be able to act wisely. The problem is there's an invisible villain in our lives. Without even being aware of it, the norms and beliefs of our unhealthy Performance and Perfection Obsessed Culture become deeply ingrained in us and affect all our thoughts, decisions, and behavior all the time.

To have any chance of ever feeling truly fulfilled—and ever feeling really good about ourselves and the life we live—we have to understand

and become aware of how this invisible villain makes us act irrationally, leaving us feeling inadequate and unfulfilled. More importantly, we need to understand it at a practical level so that we will immediately start breaking free from this pattern in our own lives no matter how hectic life might be.

Here's the good news. There's a simple way for me to help you accomplish this: through a fictional story. It's sometimes easier to see other people's challenges and irrational behavior more clearly than our own.

By following how pervasively our unhealthy culture negatively affects the different characters in the story you're about to read, you will gain a unique insight as to how this culture also influences your own life. And, by witnessing how the characters in the story break free from these effects, you'll be able to do this yourself.

None of the characters in this story are real, but all their traits and challenges are collected from actual people I have helped—or from myself. The positive changes the characters experience in the story happened in real lives.

I can almost promise that by simply reading this fictional story you will find yourself starting to automatically act more wisely and beginning to feel better about yourself and the life you live—alongside the stranded vacationers in the story.

CHAPTER 1

The Stranded Vacationers

The Getaway

I t was a dream vacation spot. A tiny island in the South Pacific, far from any mainland or even other islands. Perfect for people looking to get away from their hectic lives, to lie on the white sandy beach, drink exotic cocktails, and swim in the turquoise blue ocean.

It seemed like paradise, but it had a hidden flaw. The weather could be a problem as well as an attraction because of the unpredictable currents, the sudden high winds, and the heavy rain that could spring up out of nowhere. And the isolation of the island meant that sometimes they were cut off for days, not only from incoming transportation but even from the internet.

This group of visitors was not reacting calmly to the news that they would be on the island for several more days.

9 a.m.

"What do you mean we can't leave?" the man almost screamed at the front desk clerk. He was in his early forties, with graying hair already receding from his forehead. His face grew redder the more he gave in to his temper.

The desk clerk was patient. "I'm sorry, sir, but as you can see, the weather has deteriorated since last night's storm. Small planes can't land in these high winds and heavy rain, so we must do the best we can until the weather clears."

The man turned on his heel and strode across the lobby, shouting at his hapless wife, Barbara, to follow him.

She half-ran behind to keep up with him. "Now, Alex," she said, almost in tears, "you need to calm down. This is embarrassing!"

Alex's temper flared even higher. "How can I calm down when I'm dealing with idiots?" he shouted. "There must be a way to get off this island, and I'm going to find it. I'm not sitting around here waiting on their schedule! I'm going to get on the internet and sort out a flight for us. I'll book a private jet if I have to."

As they disappeared into the elevator, a middle-aged, fair-haired man sitting on a rattan couch in the lobby directed a sympathetic glance at the desk clerk. Dr. Krinksted wondered what would happen when Alex realized there would be no internet in this storm.

10 a.m.

A man sat at one of the low coffee tables in the outside lounge with a woman across from him. He leaned towards her, flicking open a cigarette lighter, and she took the opportunity to cup his hand in hers as she lit her cigarette.

She smiled. "Actually, I've been trying to quit—again!" said Diana. "But it's too much to try not to smoke as we sit in this godforsaken place with rain pelting down on the roof."

"I know what you mean," replied Rohan. "I wish I could get a drink. You'd think they would open the bar early since we're stuck here for a while."

"I think they will, but maybe not at 10:00 in the morning."

"I'm sorry we didn't meet before, Diana," said Rohan, "but now that we have, maybe the extra time in the hotel won't be so bad."

"Daddy! Daddy! We're not going home today. You can teach me to swim in the pool." The small figure ran across the lobby and launched herself onto Rohan's lap. He threw a rueful grimace at his companion as a woman followed the child to their table.

Her eyes sent daggers at Diana as she spoke to her husband, "I see you haven't wasted any time, as usual."

Getting the picture, Diana stood up to leave. "I daresay I'll catch you later, Rohan," she said, but her expression wasn't very promising from Rohan's point of view.

His wife, Harini, heaved a deep sigh. Clearly, Rohan's way of dealing with stress was adding to her own.

Dr. Krinksted saw trouble brewing.

Noon

The doctor was sitting at his usual table in the dining area as the other guests arrived.

Alex and Barbara took their table in the corner, anger still rolling from him in waves as she cringed silently over the menu. "You forgot your pills, dear," she almost whispered. "But don't worry. I brought them for you."

Alex ignored her as well as the pills and carried on nursing his wrath.

Rohan and Harini sat with their little girl, whose chatter fell innocently into the silence between the adults. When Diana walked into the dining area by herself, Harini stiffened while Rohan kept his eyes on the menu. Diana lit up a cigarette as she sat down, a frown detracting from her lovely face. The waiter wondered whether he was brave enough to tell her smoking wasn't allowed.

A short, round man nodded at Dr. Krinksted as he took his seat at the next table. "I sure hope they've got decent grub laid on for us while we're stuck here—and they better not think I'm paying for it either!" His action of patting his stomach seemed unconscious as he immediately began scanning the menu.

"Now, Phil," said Elinor, his stylish, blond wife. "Remember your diet. They always have some nice salads on the menu."

Phil snorted. "You have to be kidding me, Elinor," he said. "How can I stay on that stupid diet when I'm stuck here for who knows how long with a bunch of strangers?"

The waiter delivered their order, and Elinor began elegantly eating her salad. She said nothing while her husband tucked into a pile of french fries and a huge steak.

"I hope the gift shop is open," said Elinor a few minutes later. "Maybe I can find a nice silk scarf."

"My God, Elinor," Phil said loudly. "Haven't you spent enough money already in this place? Why don't you just see how long you can stay away from my wallet for a change?"

"Fine, I'll stay away from the shop as long as you stay away from all that disgusting food!" retorted Elinor. Phil didn't reply, but the mound of food seemed to have a calming effect on him.

Dr. Krinksted himself was not immune to the stress of their shared situation, but he remained calm as he chose his favorite pie with not even a twinge of guilt.

As the go-to expert regarding all the negative effects our Performance and Perfection Obsessed Culture has in people's lives, he knew how to break free from it. His latest book, *The Ultimate Life Skill,* had just become a bestseller.

His publisher had asked him to develop an online workshop based on the book, and he saw an unexpected opportunity here among these stranded vacationers.

It was clear to him they could all benefit from the information and simple training in his book, like most people in our unhealthy culture. But in this situation, Dr. Krinksted also wondered if opportunities to reach out to these people and make a win-win situation for all might arise.

Melanie

The next morning, Dr. Krinksted was having late morning coffee at a little table in the sumptuous hotel lobby, an island of serenity in the midst of agitated, frustrated people who had a hard time coping with not being able to go home.

"Hello—I'm sorry to interrupt your reading, but you're Dr. Krinksted, aren't you?"

"Yes, I am."

"I watched your interview in *Good Morning America* last week and was really intrigued by what you were saying about your book, *The Ultimate Life Skill*. I saw it in the airport, so I bought a copy. What a surprise to meet the author!"

Dr. Krinksted smiled at the young woman and asked her name.

"I'm Melanie," she replied, reaching to shake his outstretched hand. "May I join you for a few moments if you're not too busy?"

He laid his book aside and gestured for her to sit on the other chair. "How did you come to be here, Melanie?"

"I'm on vacation with my parents. We don't usually vacation together anymore, but this was supposed to be just for a few days, and it sounded like fun. I have to admit, though, I hope we get off the island soon."

"Yes, I think we're all feeling that way. How are you enjoying the book?"

"It has definitely captured my interest. I had no idea our hectic modern world had so many negative effects in so many areas of people's lives. I must say, it does resonate with me when you describe how this *always-behindness, never-enoughness* culture ends up making me feel inadequate and unfulfilled. I can't wait to get to the chapters where I'll learn your simple routines so I can start breaking free from this."

"Yes, I understand, and you're not alone with those feelings," replied Dr. Krinksted with an empathetic smile. "In our Performance and Perfection Obsessed Culture, no matter how much we are or do, we feel it's never enough. I believe it's simply wrong that the very culture we live in damages—instead of building up—our ability to feel good about who we are and the life we live. It's crazy that the biggest villain in our lives is really something we're doing to ourselves, and without even being aware of it, for the most part. But that's how culture works. It's not a coincidence that the words *culture* and *cult* have the same origin."

**No matter how much we are or do, we
feel it's never enough.**

Melanie nodded thoughtfully. "So, how did you end up so interested in this topic in the first place, Dr. Krinksted?"

"Well, when I was in my thirties, I was very successful by most objective measures. I was happily married with three healthy kids, my own private practice, and I was financially well off. But without really being aware of it, I always felt under pressure to do even better and improve something in my life. So, I started following all the contemporary thought leaders, but what was taught only helped short-term. After experiencing a high from just another great book or seminar, I quickly ended up more or less where I was before. And I met a lot of people that seemed to experience the same cycle as I did. After this happened for a couple of years, I remember specifically asking myself these questions: Why do so many people from all walks of life keep experiencing a deep yearning for something intangible, even though we're already doing really well by normal and reasonable objective standards? What is it we're not seeing or not getting right?

"Using my scientific background, I started studying this from all the perspectives I could find, from the most scientifically recognized and documented to the most alternative ideas. I slowly realized that there's an invisible villain in our lives that makes us think and act irrationally. This invisible villain is our Performance and Perfection Obsessed Culture. So, for the next couple of years, I taught myself how to slowly break away from this unhealthy culture. I experienced feeling better and better about myself and more fulfilled, not always obsessively focusing so much on what should be changed or could be improved."

Dr. Krinksted took a deep breath, noticing how excited he always became when talking about his favorite subject. He remembered that people needed time to be able to digest this information, as it was so different from what they had been ingrained with all their lives.

"And just to end my story—since then, I have made it my mission to help other people also defy this invisible villain and experience the same benefits in their lives." Dr. Krinksted just couldn't hide how much he loved his work.

The doctor noticed that Melanie looked tired, and he thought to himself that it might be because she imagined that this defiance would require a ton of work. "You look like someone just took all the energy out of your body, Melanie. But it's not complicated. You really only need to train and use one fundamental human life skill to understand how this invisible villain is messing up you and your life—and to learn to defy it. It's so simple that I can teach anybody how to incorporate this training into even the most hectic, busy life. That's why I decided to write the book."

It looked to Dr. Krinksted like Melanie had a hard time understanding the concept. This didn't come as a surprise since he knew this information had to be experienced to really grasp it, which was what his book was all about.

Melanie changed the subject. "I was pleased to see that your method is based on common sense and neuroscience. Most of what I've read is full of spiritual or new age woo-woo stuff, and I don't buy into most of that."

"Neither do I, Melanie," replied the doctor. "While I respect people's right to believe what they want, much of what is out there can, at best, temporarily relieve some of the damage that our Performance and Perfection Obsessed Culture creates in our lives. But if you don't expose and confront this invisible villain and break free from it, your need for relief will always be there under the surface. My book is based on straightforward human psychology and how our human nervous system works. *The Ultimate Life Skill* is really just that: a human skill we all have. Unfortunately, it's one that's highly undertrained and underused in our culture."

Dr. Krinksted looked behind Melanie to see a middle-aged couple coming their way.

"Melanie! So, there you are—we've been looking for you," called the woman.

Melanie turned around and jumped up. "Oh, hi Mom. Hi, Dad," she said. "Sorry about that. I ran into Dr. Krinksted here—he's the author of that book I told you about. Imagine finding he's right here in the same hotel!" She turned back to the doctor, "Dr. Krinksted, thank you so much for giving me your time and all this fascinating information. Now I'm even more keen to read the book."

Dr. Krinksted stood up, shaking hands with all three. "It was my pleasure, Melanie. I'd be happy to answer any more of your questions while we're here, although I don't know how long that will be."

"Oh, I almost forgot," said Melanie's mother. "We just came from the reception, and it will be at least two more days before we can leave. Tomorrow is Saturday, and the weekend is apparently getting in the way of restoring power."

"Then, in that case," said Dr. Krinksted, "I hope our paths will cross again."

Invitation to Meeting

Dr. Krinksted was sitting outside the hotel, experiencing the sights and smells of the hotel as they were different from the sights and smells he was used to. Suddenly, he saw his new young friend hurrying towards him across the lobby.

"I'm sorry to bother you again, Dr. Krinksted, but do you have a moment?"

"Yes, of course, Melanie. Most people call me Dr. K, so please feel free to do so."

"I just finished the introduction in your book, and, from what I understand, the very first way you help the readers understand and experience what *The Ultimate Life Skill* is, is by helping them use it to overcome a bad habit."

"Yes, that's correct, Melanie."

"And the way you help them overcome a bad habit is totally different from how we usually try to do it using our willpower?"

"Yes, also correct, Melanie. How we usually do it doesn't work most of the time. If it did, there wouldn't be anything called bad habits because we would just quit when we decided to. But we all know that's not the way it works, right?"

Melanie nodded. "So, how is it different?"

"Well, in our Performance and Perfection Obsessed Culture, we learn that we have so-called free will and that we can accomplish anything we want if we just want it bad enough and try hard enough using our willpower. But that's a fallacy. We don't have free will, and willpower isn't anything like what we have come to believe. No matter how much we want to change whatever bad habits we're struggling with or how rational or sensible we might think we are or should be, we all struggle with one or more habits we can't seem to ever overcome."

Melanie nodded, a few bad habits of her own immediately coming to mind.

"Did you read the chapter on "The Illusion of Free Will" in the book yet?"

"No, not yet. That's the very next thing I will get to," Melanie replied.

"Well, this false belief in free will lies at the foundation of most of the damage our Performance and Perfection Obsessed Culture creates in our lives. Can you see how believing deep inside that you're totally free to create exactly what you want if you just want it bad enough and try hard enough—when this isn't true—will always end up making you feel frustrated and inadequate?"

Melanie could more than see this. The feeling of not measuring up—that she knew all too well in numerous areas of her life—immediately arose in her body.

Dr. Krinksted noticed Melanie's reaction and continued, "But here's what's worse, Melanie; it doesn't stop there. Our unhealthy culture makes you act irrationally in so many other ways that are not in line with who you feel you are and what's really important for all human beings. This makes you feel even more inadequate. That's why learning to break free from this invisible villain creates such a massive positive impact in any person's life."

Melanie got back to why she interrupted Dr. Krinksted in the first place. "I must admit that one of the things that made me buy your book was because it promised to help people conquer bad habits," she said with a little grimace. "I have a terrible sweet tooth, and . . . speaking about feeling bad about myself, I hate myself for not being able to control this. Fortunately, I don't really have a weight problem, but I know this bad habit is definitely not healthy for me."

She laughed but soon became serious again as she continued, "The thing is, when I told my parents a bit about your book and the things you'd told me about, they were really intrigued. I said I was serious about working on my sweet tooth using your method, and that got them really curious because they know I've struggled with this. My dad has tried to quit smoking so many times I've lost count, and he still smokes a pack a day. He's usually quite skeptical about his ability to ever quit now, so here's what I wanted to ask you—and I hope you don't think I'm being too cheeky."

The doctor smiled, charmed by her enthusiasm.

Melanie continued, "We were wondering if you could give us a little of your time, maybe later today, and kind of guide us through your method of quitting bad habits, just so that we can be sure we're doing it right. Is that possible?"

"As a matter of fact, Melanie, it's not only possible, but it would be quite helpful to me. My publisher has asked me to develop an online workshop based on my book. This would be an opportunity for me to teach you *The Ultimate Life Skill* in a workshop setting, and I could get feedback on how it works for you, making it a win-win."

Melanie clapped her hands and smiled. "Thank you so much, Dr. Krinksted. I have to say that my dad is skeptical."

"I hear that a lot, Melanie. Most people are skeptical to begin with. Remember, we've all been indoctrinated our whole life with the idea that performance and perfection are what's most crucial in life, that we need to fight hard and struggle 24/7. Anything else is labeled as weak. I'll talk more about this when we meet."

"Excellent! Thank you so much again. When should we do it?"

"Well, I'll need half an hour for the instructions. But before that, we need to talk about *The Illusion of Free Will.* You need to know the facts about how our nervous system works to be able to get the full benefit of the training you're about to start."

Melanie interrupted, "And how long do you think that will take?"

"It's hard for me to predict because this false belief has been so deeply ingrained in us all our lives. Believing that we're 100 percent in control of our own actions—or that we should be—lies deep in most of us and is hard to shake. But an hour or so is probably enough for a start. Why don't we make it one and a half hours, so we're sure to have enough time."

Dr. Krinksted smiled. "Let's meet at 1 p.m. I'll see if I can get a little conference room for us. When you come down, just ask at reception where we are meeting. I'm excited about this, Melanie. See you soon."

*

Later that morning, Dr. Krinksted heard the ping on his phone that indicated a text message was coming in.

It was a message from Melanie: *Hi Dr. K. I was wondering if you would like a bigger group for this trial workshop? The thing is, we've been talking to some of the other guests, and a few of them would like to join us. If we can meet at 4 p.m., you should have a group of at least ten people.*

Dr. Krinksted replied immediately: *Sounds great, thanks, Melanie. And 4 p.m. is actually even better for me, and around ten is a nice size group to work with :-) I'll see if the hotel can give us a bigger conference room.*

But Melanie was ahead of him: *Already done, Dr. K—just in case you said yes, I asked at the reception. We can have Conference Room 6 on the second floor.*

Good thinking, Melanie. I look forward to seeing you all at 4 p.m. Can't wait to tell you all about the Illusion of Free Will.

Dr. Krinksted could feel the excitement in his body as he put his phone back in his pocket.

CHAPTER 2

The Illusion of Free Will

The First Session

"Good afternoon, everybody, and welcome. My name is Dr. Krinksted, and I'm the author of *The Ultimate Life Skill: How to Break Free from Our Performance and Perfection Obsessed Culture and Be More Fulfilled.* I've already run into a few of you during our enforced extended vacation here on the island, but not everyone. It would be helpful for me to know some basic information about you all, so will you please introduce yourselves briefly before we begin. Also, I'd love to know what made each of you come along today—other than passing the time while we're stuck here. Let's start on my left and go around."

The first person on his left was Melanie, and she smiled as she decided to turn around to address the group. "Hi, my name is Melanie. I'm thirty-one years old. I came here with my parents for a few days' vacation, and I happened to pick up Dr. K's book in the airport. Then I ran into him in the lobby, and he was kind enough to take time to explain some of his work to me. I'm here because I want to understand better how what he calls our Performance and Perfection Obsessed Culture messes up my life, and how I can break away from it."

"I'm Cliff, Melanie's father. I came along because she talked me into it."

Although his grin took the edge off the words, his wife shook her head as she smiled at the group. "I'm Melanie's mother, Irene. It's true, Melanie seemed so excited about what Dr. Krinksted had talked to her about that we wanted to hear more. Also, I'm a physician, and I see a lot of patients that are affected by stress, so I'm curious if there's something I can be more aware of when helping them. And I can help Melanie discern if your take on this really is based on science, as you claim. So that's why I'm here," she finished, smiling encouragingly at her daughter.

Next in line was the man Dr. Krinksted had heard complaining at the reception desk the day before. In fact, everyone had heard him! His arms were folded tightly across his chest, and his face was unsmiling as he spoke, "I'm Alex DeGroot. I don't understand why they can't manage to get us off this island, but it seems they can't, and we're stuck here for now. I've nothing better to do, so I hope you've got something worthwhile to tell us."

The meek-looking woman beside him seemed embarrassed at her husband's rudeness as she spoke quietly, "I'm Alex's wife, Barbara."

"Hi all," said the next person. "I'm Rohan Singh, and this is my wife, Harini. We're here with our daughter; she's in the children's club right now."

A stylish-looking blond woman in her forties was next. "I'm Elinor Walsh, and this is my husband Phil," she said, indicating the chair next to her. Our kids are in the children's club as well; we have a six-year-old girl and a twelve-year-old boy."

In contrast to his wife's fashionable appearance, Phil looked thrown together in too-tight jeans that sat low under his belly. "I'm here because she dragged me along," he said with an unpleasant smile.

Two young women were next. "I'm Laura, and this is my fiancée Hannah," pointing to the woman next to her. "I'm twenty-four years old and doing my master's in psychology. I'm here because Melanie told me that you had written a book that claimed there's one life skill that's fundamental and crucial above all others and that this training will make the biggest positive impact in people's lives with the smallest amount of effort. Given my studies, I'm interested to hear what this is all about now that I have the chance. Also, she mentioned that you talk about what you call our Performance and Perfection Obsessed Culture. I haven't heard this expression before, but it does resonate with me, and I would like to hear more about what you mean by that."

Laura's fiancée, Hannah, seemed shy and just raised her hand and said, "Hi," without really looking around at the other people.

"I'm Jill," the next person said, "and I'm traveling alone with my two daughters. Yes, thank God for the children's club. If it wasn't for them, I wouldn't be able to feel I've had any little bit of vacation, nor would I be here now."

After an elderly guy named Yan had introduced himself, an attractive redheaded woman at the end of the row was last to speak. "Hi everybody. I'm Diana, and I came along out of curiosity—and if it's of any interest, I'm here by myself."

Dr. Krinksted recognized the woman who had been the object of Rohan's attentions in the lobby before his wife showed up. He didn't miss the glare directed at her by Elinor Walsh. He thought it was just as well she was at the far end of the row. "Thank you everybody, and by the way, please call me Dr. K. To reach more people, my publisher has asked me to create a workshop based on my book. So, on top of hopefully helping each of you make a big positive impact in your lives, I hope our time together will give me an opportunity for some feedback on the workshop format I'll be using with you. I'm grateful to you all for coming, and I'll do my best to make it worth your while."

He smiled at the interesting group of people—some of whom smiled back.

The Illusion of Free Will

"All right, now that I know you all a little bit more, let's delve into the material. The big passion in my life has always been to understand what it takes for us as human beings to feel truly fulfilled.

"Years back, I realized that there's one villain, second to none, hindering this. The problem is that most people don't know of this villain—not to mention how to break free from it. So, because of this invisible villain, millions of people are left constantly questioning themselves and the life they live. They have a sense that life is often flying by too quickly, instead of feeling good about who they are and the life they live.

"The invisible villain I'm talking about is our Performance and Perfection Obsessed Culture."

Dr. Krinksted looked around to make sure he had people's attention as he continued, "After coming to this realization and learning how to break free myself, I started my search on how to help other people see and understand how this villain affects their lives so massively and how they could also break free. After a few years, I realized that I could teach this skill in a simple way that could be easily incorporated in even the most hectic, busy lives. That's when I decided to write my book."

Dr. Krinksted couldn't hide his excitement. "Okay, so to be able to really understand how our culture can be such a villain in your lives, you need to understand one of the most fundamental false beliefs in our unhealthy culture. I call it the *Illusion of Free Will.*"

There was a little stir of interest in the room, some leaning forward on their chairs.

"We've all grown up with the belief that we are 100 percent responsible for our actions, implying that we have free choice about what to do in any and all circumstances—that whatever we did, we could always have simply chosen not to do it. Would you agree?"

A few of the faces took on a puzzled expression, while others nodded.

"Well," said Dr. Krinksted, "a short version of this is that we believe that as human beings we have what is called free will. But I'm here to tell you that's an illusion. The truth is that, for the most part, what we do in any given moment is controlled by parts of our nervous systems that we're not in control of and mostly not even aware of.

"Now, I'm going to give you the layman's neuroscientific explanation of why we don't actually have a so-called free will at all, why we often can't help doing something, even when we have decided not to."

No matter how sensible or educated you are, most of what you do is not really by conscious choice.

"Now just a minute," Alex interrupted in his belligerent tone. "What do you mean we're not in control and can't be held responsible? Are you telling me I'm not in control of myself? Are you saying I shouldn't hold people accountable for their stupid behavior?" His face was growing redder, and he wore an angry scowl.

Dr. Krinksted answered him calmly, "Yes, to a certain extent I am, Alex. The idea of free will is an illusion. The problem is it's such an integral part of the cultural belief system that it has become deeply ingrained in us as a truth. So, we tend to downplay the instances that disprove the idea of free will.

"Our typical explanation is that we lack willpower or have no backbone, but that's not the whole truth. I know it's not what we learn growing up, and that our culture is—to a large degree—built on a belief in free will, so I understand it can be disturbing to hear that it's not reality. The truth is that we all have a certain percentage of actions that we can't help taking, even though we know we shouldn't be doing them for some reason: because they're not healthy for us, or because they're not in line with who we think we should be or what we really want. No matter how sensible or educated you are, most of what you do is not really by conscious choice. And in maybe 1, 5, or 10 percent of your actions, you end up acting in a way you really don't want to or even have decided not to act. That's just how our human nervous system works. No wonder so many people feel somewhat inadequate and frustrated when believing in this illusion while experiencing their own actions that are regularly *unwise* to say the least."

He could see they were having some trouble absorbing this news, and Alex had a thunderous look on his face. "The truth is that if you want to break free from all the challenges and problems caused by our Performance and Perfection Obsessed Culture and start being more fulfilled in life, you need to fully understand the concept of free will—what's true and what's not. It's not that it's all wrong—it's just not all right."

"Okay, that's it!" mumbled Alex, jumping to his feet. "I've heard enough of this rubbish. I'm leaving."

Dr. Krinksted looked at Alex. "Of course, you're free to leave if you want, Alex, but will you let me tell you a story before you go? It's something that will put the notion of free will in a different—and more correct light. Remember, all I'm telling you is based on neuroscience."

Something about Dr. Krinksted's calm response seemed to take the wind out of Alex's sails, and he even gave a sheepish grin. "Well, it's not as if I've got anywhere else to be. Okay, tell me your story."

Dr. Krinksted began, "In 1990, a ship caught fire in Danish waters, creating a catastrophe that eventually killed 159 people. In an interview years later, one of the survivors told the story of his last minutes on the ship. It was a story that had haunted him for years.

"He told of running up the stairs to get away from the fire, all the while pushing other passengers aside in his desperate attempt to save himself. Looking back, he knew that some of these people might have lost their lives because of his actions.

"Here's my question to you. Did this man act out of free will that day? Did he have true freedom of choice about how to act when running up those stairs to save his life?"

Without waiting for anyone else to speak, Alex jumped in, "No, of course not," he almost shouted. His wife seemed to shrink with embarrassment as he continued, "When something like that happens, we all react by reflex. If any of us were caught up in a situation like that, I think our natural reaction would be the same as this poor guy's—save ourselves without being able to worry about anybody else."

"But if that's the case, Alex," said Dr. Krinksted, "do we really have free will?"

"Yes, of course we do, because most of us never end up in horrible situations like that. In normal situations, I do have free will, and it's my own fault if I act in a stupid way. I just have to pull myself together. I hate people that play the victim, and that's what you're telling us to do!"

Dr. Krinksted ignored the last part of Alex's rant. "So, you agree that in certain situations we might act instinctively, not being able to stop and think before acting out of what could be called free will?"

"I suppose so, in extreme circumstances like the one in your story."

"Do you agree that when our brains pick up signs of great danger, something other than our free will takes over?"

"Sure. I don't think anybody would argue against that." Alex was beginning to calm down as he saw where Dr. Krinksted's argument was taking him—although he wasn't quite ready to admit it yet.

"I assume you know what a phobia is," said Dr. Krinksted, addressing Alex again.

"Yes, of course. My wife is terrified of spiders."

His wife flinched a little, taken aback by suddenly becoming part of Alex's confrontation with the doctor.

"What about you, Alex? Do you suffer from any phobias?" Dr. Krinksted asked.

"No, I don't."

"Is there anything you're more afraid of than you think you should be? Anything at all?"

"We-e-ll," said Alex reluctantly, "what comes to mind is giving presentations at work. Just before I stand up, I usually have this massive lump in my throat." Now that he had publicly spoken about what he considered a weakness, Alex reverted to his bluff manner. "So, what's your point?"

"Here's my point," said Dr. Krinksted. "You're right in both instances. There's a mechanism in our brains that starts shutting off our ability to reason as soon as it picks up what might be signs of danger, allowing us to react quickly and instinctively. You're also right regarding your fear of public speaking—which is in fact a phobia. In medical terms it's called *glossophobia*."

Alex opened his mouth, but Dr. Krinksted hurried on before he could speak. "You see, our nervous system makes mistakes, perceiving danger when it's not really there and intervenes in our ability to reason in order to make us act more quickly. For example, when your wife sees a harmless spider or when you have to give a speech at a social gathering, objectively there's no actual danger, but your ability to reason will be reduced, nonetheless.

"What you all must understand is that this happens more often than most people are aware of. In fact it happens all the time, to some degree. This mechanism in your brain is not an on/off switch—it's more like the volume control knob on a radio. Depending on how severe your nervous system interprets or misinterprets the danger to be, the imaginary knob in your brain can be turned smoothly from a situation in which you have 100 percent of your reasoning available to one in which you have almost no reasoning available at all, or any level in between.

"In the case of the passenger on the ship, the knob was turned all the way down to zero, a setting in which he had no reasoning available at all and was left to act 100 percent instinctively. But later, when the danger was over and he was safe, his reasoning power came back up to 100 percent. He felt ashamed of his behavior because he didn't understand that he had no power to act any differently during those last moments on the ship."

"Okay" said Alex with a grin that was surprisingly charming. "I guess you've got me interested now, so I'll sit down again."

When not able to be nice, happy, positive, and effective all the time, we feel something is wrong with us.

"Thanks, Alex. I appreciate that. My only objective here is to help you all understand and experience how our nervous systems are making us do irrational things, and I wouldn't tell you all this if it wasn't absolutely critical for you to understand. Here's the thing, because the illusion of free will is deeply ingrained in us, when we experience not being in control—not able to be nice, happy, positive, and effective all the time—we feel something is wrong with us. And when we feel something is wrong with us, we become scared, and no matter if our fear is based on real danger or not, the connections to the rational parts of our brain are impaired."

Dr. Krinksted took a deep breath, recognizing his own tendency to get worked up over this subject, and before he could speak again, Laura raised her hand.

"Are you saying that we don't have free will because we can lose access to the more rational parts of our brains?"

"Yes, that's correct, Laura, and we have to talk about one more thing to get all the way around this false concept of free will. We have to talk about willpower, which I briefly mentioned a minute ago. If the notion of free will were true, we would always have enough willpower to do exactly what we want to do—what our will wants us to do. We all know this isn't true, both from our own experiences and from looking at each other. There's always a fight in us between what we want to do—our will—and the pull from the more primitive parts of our nervous system. The more primitive parts of our nervous system always have the largest impact because they control how many of the connections to the rational parts of our brain are open or not. And it's in the rational parts of our brains that our willpower is located. This is, of course, an oversimplification, but for all practical purposes, that's how it works and all you have to know to achieve all the benefits from this training you're about to start.

"So, to sum up again—when our nervous system interprets danger, no matter if objectively there's danger or not, our ability to reason and use our willpower becomes impaired. And when our nervous systems don't interpret anything as dangerous at any given moment, our ability to reason and use our willpower is not impaired. In the latter situations, the concept of free will seems more true, but it's still just an illusion.

"Let me just repeat and emphasize one last thing here before we move on. There's a perfectly good reason for this mechanism in our brains—because it makes us able to react instinctively to save time, which is sometimes essential to keep us alive. The problem is that when logic and reasoning become impaired when there's no real danger, we end up not being able to act reasonably or wise, for no good reason. This reality is what you'll start experiencing soon regarding bad habits. I might be getting ahead of myself, but does that answer your question, Laura?"

Dr. Krinksted looked not only on Laura but on everybody in the room to see how it landed.

Laura replied, "So, isn't what you're pointing to how self-control works? We all want self-control but know that there are situations where it's hard or impossible to control ourselves. And what you're describing is what ends up taking over the control when we lose it, right? And that believing in the illusion of free will would be the same as believing that we always have 100 percent control over ourselves?"

Dr. Krinksted smiled. "Yes, Laura, that's spot on. It's really just different ways of saying the same thing. Maybe thinking about this from a *who's really in control* perspective might make it easier to understand, because most of us experience that we're definitely not always in 100 percent control of ourselves."

Jill, the woman travelling with her two daughters, spoke up from the back of the room, "Is this related to what we call being *triggered*?"

"Yes, being triggered is the extreme end in which you lose all your self-control. Do you have experience of being triggered, Jill?"

"Yes, all the time! My daughters are thirteen and eight. When they start teasing each other, I react quite strongly—typically yelling at them—and it's like my reaction happens almost before I have any thoughts about how to react. It feels like I've lost all control over myself, just like the man on the ship you just told us about. I call that being triggered."

"Yes, it's the same mechanism that's behind what we call being triggered, Jill. If you were able to pause and observe in slow motion what happens in your body the split second your daughters start the teasing and before you react, you would experience your body cut the connection to the rational part of your brain, creating the experience

27

of losing control—as you're describing. The problem is that contrary to working with a bad habit, this all happens so quickly that it's extremely hard to pause and just observe what is happening without doing something to make the situation go away—which in your case means yelling at your daughters. But you'll get there later on in the training."

Jill frowned a little.

Laura jumped in, "So, are you saying Jill should just let the teasing go on?" It was already obvious to everyone that Laura was the type of person that loved to explore a deeper understanding of things.

"No, that's not what I'm saying at all. There are a lot of variables in a situation like this, and I'm sure there are some difficult choices to make on how to act wisely. What I am saying is that when your rational mind has been cut off, your willpower is compromised, and your choice about how to act is diminished. Getting to a place where we experience having what I call *true freedom of choice* in everything we do is the central theme in everything you're going to learn here."

"So," interrupted Harini unexpectedly, "could it be that Jill doesn't always have to react the same way when her daughters start teasing each other? I mean, sometimes it might be best to intervene, and other times, it might be better to let them handle it themselves."

"Yes, exactly, Harini," said Dr. Krinksted. "I call it being able to act wisely, where wisely is not referring to a certain action in itself, but referencing whether an action leads to the outcome you want to create. When you increase your proficiency at *The Ultimate Life Skill,* you'll become able to act more wisely instead of irrationally. This includes being able to break free from our Performance and Perfection Obsessed Culture when that's the wise thing to do. The reason I say *when it's the wise thing to do* is because focusing on performance and perfection is not bad in itself. Wanting to do our best and making our own and other people's lives better are normal and healthy human character traits. It's the obsession part that's the villain."

"Wow," said Jill. "So, what is this ultimate life skill you're referring to?"

"I'll have to get back to that, Jill. First, I need you all to have your initial experience of what happens when the connection to the rational parts of your brains ends up being cut off. And we'll use one of your bad habits to give you that experience—which will simultaneously enable you to break that habit. I hope that sounds good?"

Everybody nodded.

CHAPTER 3

How to Overcome Bad Habits
Without Relying on Willpower

"Okay," said Dr. Krinksted, rubbing his hands together enthusiastically. "For you to get any value out of this training, you needed the background information about how your nervous system works, especially how the concept of free will is an illusion. Now that you have that, let's start increasing your proficiency of *The Ultimate Life Skill*. Teaching you how to overcome a bad habits without relying on willpower is where we'll start."

Dr. Krinksted smiled, obviously enjoying himself. "In our Performance and Perfection Obsessed Culture, the usual way of trying to overcome bad habits is through the use of willpower, right?"

People nodded.

Dr. Krinksted continued with another question, "But you've all already found that often doesn't work very well, right?"

"You got that right, Doc," said Cliff. "I've tried to quit smoking that way, but either it doesn't work for anybody, or I've got the weakest willpower in the world."

Many people in the group nodded and laughed. Clearly nobody was going to argue in favor of willpower.

"Great!" said Dr. Krinksted. "I'm glad we cleared that up right away. What you're going to experience here is actually, in slow motion, how your willpower is being undermined by something more powerful every time you give in to your bad habit. Just like we've talked about. But you'll also experience how to prevent this undermining of your willpower from happening, making you able to overcome your bad habit slowly but surely.

"The first thing I want you to do now is identify a bad habit you'd like to work on. We all have habits we'd like to change, so you needn't be shy, although you won't need to make your habits public if you don't want to. I've given each of you pen and paper, so take a few moments to write down as many habits you can think of that you'd like to change. Make the list as long as you like for the next few minutes."

Silence fell as everyone, even those Dr. Krinksted had thought might be reluctant, began to write. After a few minutes, they had all finished.

"Okay, it seems you've all run out of bad habits," said Dr. Krinksted with a smile. "The next step is to isolate the habit you'll be working on using this method. To make it easier, I recommend you write your bad habit as a rule you'd like to follow but haven't been able to, and phrase it so that you will immediately recognize the bad habit when the urge to indulge in it strikes."

All eyes were on Dr. Krinksted as he picked up a blue marker from beneath the whiteboard at the end of the room and began to write as he spoke.

"Here are some examples of how you could phrase it:

Don't smoke before noon instead of *smoke less.*

Eat only one piece of cake with afternoon coffee instead of *eat less cake.*

Don't eat potato chips at home unless I have company instead of *eat less potato chips.*

Don't spend more than five minutes at a time on social media instead of *spend less time on social media.*

"Can you see how each of these are readily identifiable? So, each time you feel the urge to do whatever your thing is, you'll recognize it as the habit you're working on. Any questions about that?"

As nobody spoke, he continued, "All right, I'll give you five minutes now to write down the bad habit you'll work on this way. Be as specific as possible, including the timing aspect. If you have any questions, just raise your hand."

It didn't take long for everyone to finish, and the doctor asked if anyone would be willing to share the habit they had chosen. There was some reluctance, which didn't surprise him. These people were, after all, strangers to one another, and some wouldn't find it easy to disclose any personal information, let alone bad habits. But soon Melanie spoke up in her usual cheerful way.

"Well, you already know mine. My bad habit is eating too many sweets, so my desired behavior is to eat no more than two pieces of chocolate or candy a day."

Cliff grinned at his daughter. "Good luck with that, Mel!"

Several of the group laughed.

"Okay, then I'll follow my girl," he said. "I'm going to aim for your first example, Dr. K—not smoking before noon. If I can hold out till noon, that will be better than I've ever managed before."

Rohan spoke up, "I'll check my business inbox only four times a day—at 9 and 11 a.m. and 2 and 4:30 p.m."

"Good one, Rohan," said Alex. "As far as I'm concerned, all these new messaging services are a terrible invention, and anything we can do to get them under control is good. Maybe something like this could stop me from throwing my computer at the wall, which I've often been tempted to do."

Nobody quite knew how to respond to that, having all seen Alex's temper in action numerous times during their stay.

As the others didn't seem to want to share their designated habits, Dr. Krinksted decided it was time to move on and give this group of people their first taste of the simple routine he had invented.

The 3 Minute/3 Step Routine

Now that they had each zeroed in on the habit they wanted to change, the group began to be more engaged, and Dr. Krinksted knew he now had their full attention—at least for the moment. His experience told him that the simplicity of this routine sometimes made people doubt its effectiveness, so he wanted to make sure they would quickly experience what he had promised them, so that success would encourage them to continue.

"Okay," he began, "So, the purpose of what you're going to do now is twofold:

1. Giving you a conscious experience of what happens when your willpower fades away and why this happens.
2. Giving you the tool to stop that from happening, so you'll be able to act more wisely. In this case, being able to overcome your bad habit.

"You'll achieve both of these goals through training and using a simple and short routine. I call it the *3 Minute/3 Step Routine*—or in short, the *3/3 Routine*—because it is three steps that can be done in three minutes."

"That's cute," said the irrepressible Melanie. "Easy to remember."

Dr. Krinksted continued, "Let me start by giving you an overview of the three steps you'll be following." He handed out a piece of paper to everybody.

**The 3 Minute/3 Step Routine for
Overcoming Bad Habits**

Step 1: Stop and observe
Take a deep breath through your nose and observe any tension or uncomfortable sensations in your body.

Step 2: Pause and observe
Pause and observe what happens to the tension or uncomfortable sensations in your body. Don't try to change anything; just observe.

Step 3: Continue and observe
Give in to the bad habit as you normally would and observe what happens to the tension or uncomfortable sensations in your body.

Dr. Krinksted read from the paper and expanded on each step. "Every time you feel an urge to indulge in any of the activities you've defined as a bad habit, the first step is to stop and observe. When you become aware that you are about to do any of the behaviors you've listed as your bad habit, I want you to stop in that moment, take a deep breath through your nose, and observe what is happening in your body. I especially want you to look for tension or uncomfortable sensations you'd like to change or make go away.

"The second step in the 3 Minute/3 Step Routine is to observe how the tension or uncomfortable sensations you observed in step 1 might be growing in intensity or if new unpleasant sensations are emerging in your body while you resist indulging in your bad habit.

"Since I'm sure you've all tried many times to resist the urge to indulge in your bad habits with variating success, I want to underline that the 3 Minute/3 Step Routine is not a training of your willpower, but your ability to observe.

"So, in this step 2 of the 3/3 Routine, I want you to pause as long as you feel like while just observing. Don't try to change anything; just observe what is happening in your body. And while you pause, I want you to take some deep breaths as this will help you in this endeavor. Under normal circumstances, when you're not doing this 3/3 Routine, you would often end up giving in. If you didn't end up giving in more often than you would like, you wouldn't call it a bad habit in the first place, right? In step 3 of the 3 Minute/3 Step Routine, you'll give in to your bad habit as you normally would but with one crucial difference: while and after giving in, I want you to keep observing what is happening in your body and how the strength of any tension or uncomfortable sensations in your body might be decreasing or changing, especially those that you wanted to change or make go away in the previous steps."

The 3 Minute/3 Step Routine is not a training of your willpower, but your ability to observe.

"So, when you don't feel like pausing any longer, give in to your bad habit as you normally would, but keep observing what is happening in your body. Does the tension or sensations of whatever bad habit you're working on change? For example, for you Cliff, what happens in your body when you light the cigarette and inhale the smoke? And for you, Melanie, what happens in your body when you eat the chocolate or candy? Keep observing what is happening in your body for as long as you'd like while going back and continuing what you were doing before you started this 3/3 Routine. And next time you have the urge to indulge in any of the activities you've defined as your bad habit, you'll simply start the 3/3 Routine again at step 1. Does anyone have any questions?"

Alex seemed irritated and was the first to speak up. "That's it?" he asked. "That's all there is to it?"

Dr. Krinksted smiled. "Yes, that's it, Alex. I know it's simple, but please don't judge it until you try it. Remember, this is based on neuroscience, and it does work. You just have to give it a chance."

"How long should we resist in step 2?" Laura asked.

"There's no set time for this, Laura. Pausing for just a few seconds is fine, and if you feel like pausing for a longer time, that's fine too. Remember, giving in is not a sign of failure, but just another opportunity to become more fully aware of the tension and sensations in your body and how they affect you.

"Let me underline again that this is not a training of your willpower; it's about noticing something that has always happened in your body. You just haven't been aware of it before. I know it will probably be a stretch to focus only on what you experience instead of trying to resist the behavior—because the default in our Performance and Perfection Obsessed Culture is to make this moment a test of willpower as we've all been conditioned to do as we grew up. The trouble is, if you start feeling that you're not doing it right or not living up to expectations, this is fear-in-disguise. And this fear-in-disguise will cut off the connections to the rational parts of your brain and undermine your ability to use your awareness. And this, in turn, will make it harder for you to experience what you haven't noticed before, which is the primary goal of this 3/3 Routine. Does that help?"

Laura nodded thoughtfully.

"Also, if you don't happen to have time or energy for the whole routine, you can just skip step 2 and jump directly from step 1 to step 3. In that case, remember to observe the tension and sensations in your body at steps 1 and 3."

"But what if we don't ever feel like pausing at all?" asked Alex, not quite so belligerently as usual.

"That's unlikely, Alex," replied the doctor, "because you want to change. But if it does happen, just go ahead and give in—but always observing what is happening in your body as you do."

Alex nodded. "So, what you're saying is that it's almost impossible to feel we're doing this wrong. That's definitely different from what we're used to."

Barbara looked sideways at her husband, almost afraid to believe he was being so receptive to this idea. *Perhaps there really was a chance he could change*, she thought.

"If you only ever did steps 1 and 3, closely observing the tension and sensations at each step, you would still be training your ability to notice what happens in your body, which is what will ultimately lead to the results you want."

There was silence for a little while, and Dr. Krinksted let it stretch out because he knew they were processing what he had just told them.

The little pause gave the inquisitive and curious Laura enough space for another question. "Can you put some more words on what we're trying to notice?"

"Sure, and thanks for reminding me to elaborate some more on that, Laura." Dr. Krinksted realized that he had jumped a little too quickly over this, so he made a mental note.

"Bad habits are driven by cravings. If there were no such things as cravings, there wouldn't be bad habits because we simply wouldn't do what we didn't want to do. So, you'll be looking for cravings in your body. What I can tell you up front is that it's always some kind of tension or sensations in your body that you would like or need to change or make go away, because that's what your bad habit accomplishes—it makes those uncomfortable feelings we call cravings go away. That's why you've had such a hard time overcoming your bad habit.

"What you'll be searching for in the 3/3 Routine are the specific tensions and sensations of your specific bad habit as it manifests in *your body*. Cravings could be specific sensations from your mouth or throat, tension in your chest, or a general and subtle undefinable restlessness in your body. Another way to put it is that you want to expose any tension or sensations in your body when you experience the urge to indulge in your bad habit—no matter what these tension and sensations, these cravings, feel like for you. And make special note on how all these might change in step 3, when you give in to your bad habit. Does that answer your question, Laura?"

Laura still seemed somewhat confused. "Yes, and I think I have to try it to really understand what you're talking about." She smiled.

"Exactly," resumed Dr. Krinksted. "Here's what I'd like to do if you agree: We know we will be here for at least two more full days. I am willing to give you another session each day at the same time, if at least some of you would like to join me. That will give us time to work through quite a bit more of my book and still give most of you time between to try the routine out for yourself. What do you think?"

"I'm in, Doc," said Cliff, quickly joined by his wife and daughter. One by one, the others nodded or raised their hands, and Dr. Krinksted was pleased to see he would have a full group, at least for the next session.

"Excellent! The purpose of this first stage is to simply start recognizing and identifying these tensions and sensations you've had before but never really noticed or examined closely. We will meet tomorrow, and even in that short time, you'll have had some experience with the routine.

"Again, though, please remember this is not training to strengthen your willpower, so don't bang your head for not pausing long enough or at all. As long as you are becoming more aware of what is happening in your body around the habit you're addressing, you are succeeding. By doing the routine for just a few minutes every time you have one of your urges, within a couple of weeks, you might already start finding yourself resisting the cravings a little bit longer without even trying. And if you continue the training, you'll eventually reach the point of freely choosing when to give in to your craving or not without struggling at all—at which point it will no longer be a bad habit. Why this happens we'll discuss in one of our next meetings when you've all had some experiences practicing the 3/3 Routine.

"Any more questions?" The doctor looked at the group. "Okay then, thank you all for joining me in this training. I look forward to seeing you all tomorrow and learning how you make out with this simple routine."

The Second Session

Dr. Krinksted purposely didn't arrive at the meeting room until a minute or so before the start time because he wanted the participants to have an opportunity to chat among themselves and get to know each other a little better. He was pleased to see that all fourteen had returned for the second session.

After the last session, Dr. Krinksted had gone back to his room and made a few notes about each of the participants in the group so that he would be able to remember who was who, including each of their stories, questions, and challenges. He took out this piece of paper and put it on the table in front of him.

Notes:

Melanie, Melanie's mother, Irene, and Melanie's father, Cliff

Melanie

Thirty-one years old.

The enthusiastic young woman who reached out to me and initiated our group meeting. Bought the book because she wants to break a bad habit.

But also wants to better understand how our Performance and Perfection Obsessed Culture messes up her life, and how she can break away from it more. Likes that it's all based on neuroscience.

Bad habit: Has a sweet tooth.

Irene, Melanie's mother

Showed up to support her daughter. She is a physician, and she wants to make sure what her daughter is *into* is something sound and rational. As a physician, she's also open to learning something new that might allow her to better help the stressed patients in her clinic.

Cliff, Melanie's father

Told us that his daughter, Melanie, talked him into joining.

Bad habit: Smoking.

Has tried to quit many times but never succeeded. This is what he's using the 3/3 Routine to work on.

Alex and Barbara

They are probably in their forties.

Alex

The guy I heard complaining at the reception desk. He said he showed up because he didn't have anything better to do. He generally seems to have a bad temper, and he's very skeptical. He was the one who almost left when I mentioned the notion that free will is an illusion. I think he might be more stressed than he is aware of, and I got the impression that he's not very open to trying to see things in a new way no matter how true or wise they are.

Barbara

Didn't say much. Seemed embarrassed by Alex's temper and behavior.

Rohan and Harini

They are here with their young daughter.

Rohan

The guy I saw sitting in the lobby flirting with a woman when his wife and daughter entered. He did the introduction of his wife.

Bad habit: Checking his inbox all the time.

Harini

Didn't say much.

Diana

The red-haired woman who was the object of Rohan's attentions in the lobby. She is travelling by herself.

<u>Elinor and Phil</u>

The stylish, blond woman and the man that I saw in the dining area that had the discussion about her shopping and his eating habits.

They have a six-year-old girl and a twelve-year-old boy.

At the meeting, I felt tension between them.

Elinor

Introduced both of them.

Phil

Said that Elinor dragged him along to our meeting.

<u>Laura and Hannah</u>

The young couple.

Laura

The inquisitive one who is doing a master's in psychology.

Hannah

Didn't say much. Was introduced by her fiancée, Laura.

Jill

The woman who asked the question about being triggered when her two young daughters tease each other. She's alone with them here on vacation.

Yan

The oldest guy who sat in the back. Didn't share anything yet.

"Hello everyone," Dr. Krinksted began, and the chatter gradually stopped. "How have you all weathered yet another day of confinement?"

"I have to say," began Elinor, "yesterday wasn't quite so bad. It might have something to do with the fact that they've told us we can probably leave in two more days, but I actually think the content of your presentation and practicing the 3 Minute/3 Step Routine helped."

"Yes, me too," said her husband, Phil—which surprised everyone, as Phil had seemed uninterested the previous day. "I tried the exercise a few times yesterday before reaching for a bag of potato chips or a second burger. I think I kind of got it."

"That's great, Phil," said the doctor. "I'm glad to hear it. Anybody else want to share their experience?"

"Sure," said Cliff. "I've been smoking since I was sixteen, and I've tried to quit many times. Like most smokers, I've done it the typical way by stopping cold turkey from one moment to the next—I guess that's taking the willpower route you talked about yesterday. I've usually managed to quit for a time, sometimes even a couple of weeks. But then before I knew it, I was right back to smoking a pack a day again. It never made sense to me why this always happened until you told us about the illusion of free will and how our nervous system really works."

"Yes, that's the story we all know so well, Cliff—both looking at others and from trying to overcome our own bad habits," Dr. Krinksted replied. "So, what was it like for you not to try to use your willpower and just experience what was happening in your body when you had your craving?"

"It was quite interesting, actually. For the first half-minute or so I was just aware of the urge as I usually am. I also realized that a lot of the time when I have a cigarette, I don't actually have a craving at all. I guess I just reach for one before the cravings get too bad without even thinking. But yesterday, after the first minute or so, I noticed some tension building up just as you described. For me, it was in my chest. But I also became aware of a lot of mind chatter going on in my head around quitting. It seems as if part of me is saying I should resist, while another part is trying to convince me that it's not that bad and that I can quit later."

"Yes, that's typically how our thoughts behave. When we start noticing them, we realize that we're talking to ourselves all the time. Did anyone else have the same experience?"

Several heads nodded in agreement.

"What happened after that, Cliff? When you gave in and started inhaling the smoke in step 3, did you notice a change in the tension and sensations in your body?"

"Oh, yes! As soon as I took the first puff, I felt my body relax. It felt really good; all the tension and uncomfortable sensations in my body related to the craving stopped. The inner dialogue also stopped, but just for a moment. Then another voice started telling me how weak and stupid I was."

"Yes, if we are forced to stay here longer than two more days, we'll talk more about how this inner dialogue we all have is such a huge part of how our Performance and Perfection Obsessed Culture messes us and our lives up."

Melanie spoke up, "I can totally relate to that, Dad. I experienced something similar when I did the 3/3 when having the urge for eating sweets. But there was one time I didn't give in. I felt like tolerating the discomfort in my body, and after a while, it just seemed to go away. I'm not sure how to express this, but it was as if just experiencing the discomfort kind of prevented it from taking over. Does that make sense, Dr. K?"

"Yes, it does, Melanie. You see, when you consciously confront the tension and sensations we're talking about here, your nervous system learns by experience that although they feel unpleasant and are something you'd like to go away, they're definitely not a sign of real danger! As a result, you slowly become more and more able to tolerate those sensations without really having to try. Without having to use a lot of willpower, so to speak."

The doctor knew it might take some of them a little more time to experience these tensions and sensations and to really understand what he was pointing to, and he gave them a few seconds to take this information in before he spoke again.

"Understanding and experiencing this lays the foundation for you to be able to break free from our unhealthy culture. I'll be diving into it more deeply when you've had more experience of consciously exposing and confronting what happens in your body, rather than immediately doing something that changes or numbs any tension or sensation without becoming consciously aware of it. Did anyone experience anything different from the 3 Minute/3 Step Routine?"

"Yes, I think I did," said Harini thoughtfully.

Rohan looked at his wife in surprise, as she hadn't really seemed that interested in this whole thing. At least, she hadn't said anything about it.

"I have to say I couldn't really understand what I was supposed to notice. I just struggled to resist as usual."

"Don't worry, Harini. That's actually a great observation in itself, and it should make it easier for you to do the training now. Can I ask: What was the bad habit you were working on?"

"I've been a nail biter ever since I was a kid and have never been able to shake the habit. My mother used to put something on my nails that tasted nasty so I wouldn't bite them, and my father gave me pocket money every time he could cut my nails. I still couldn't resist biting them. I hate myself for this, and I hide my nails from other people because I'm embarrassed of my lack of self-control."

"Yes, bad habits often do that to us. They make us feel bad about ourselves. But don't worry, Harini. Even though this might sound strange, simply noticing that you weren't sure what to notice means you actually stopped and started noticing something new. I'll say you're off to a good start."

Harini smiled shyly and looked sideways at her husband. Surprising even himself, Rohan reached out and squeezed her hand.

As there were no more comments, Dr. Krinksted asked if everyone wanted to continue the training and meet again the next day. There was some questioning and chatter, but everyone said they did.

Private Chat with Jill

The next morning, Dr. Krinksted looked up from his coffee to see a woman from his group coming into the lounge area. She saw him, but appeared hesitant to approach, so he smiled encouragingly. She smiled back and came over to where he was sitting.

"Hi, Dr. Krinksted. Is it okay if I take a minute of your time?" she asked.

"Of course," he replied, "and please call me Dr. K."

Jill smiled.

"You're the one who asked the question about being triggered, aren't you?"

"Yes, that's me. What you've been telling us about the illusion of free will makes so much sense to me, but I didn't want to talk in more detail about my problem in front of the group—at least not yet. Would you mind if I just asked you a quick question? I want to make sure I'm getting this right."

"Yes, of course."

"Well, it's true that I get triggered when my daughters tease each other, but that's just the tip of the iceberg. The truth is, I always seem to be yelling at them for something. I know I shouldn't—they're just kids being kids after all. But I can't seem to stop myself. Here's my question. Can I consider my yelling a bad habit and work on it the same way as Cliff with his smoking or Phil with his eating habits?"

"Yes, you can, Jill—and you're actually spot on with your understanding. The mechanism behind your yelling at the kids is much the same as it is for what we call bad habits. When your kids behave in a certain way, discomfort you're not aware of immediately builds up in your body. Since yelling is your nervous system's way of reducing or eliminating that tension, the knob we've talked about automatically turns up to the point where your willpower becomes impaired, and you're left to act instinctively yelling at your kids even though you don't want to."

Jill nodded rapidly, a little frown on her face. "Yes, that's exactly what it feels like. It's like I am suddenly just yelling without choosing to do so."

"I'll be going into this in more depth with the group. The only reason I haven't yet is that it's a much more difficult situation to use the 3 Minute/3 Step Routine because in situations like the one you describe, it all happens so quickly—almost instantly—and you're not in control of when to give in. Unlike, for example, an urge to reach out for a cigarette. Starting with bad habits is the easiest way for most people to gain a first experience of this mechanism and what these tensions and sensations feel like for them. We could call it a stepping stone to using the routine in more and more complex life situations, which will ultimately enable you to act more wisely in all areas of life."

"I'm glad you said that, Dr. K, because I couldn't really think of a typical bad habit to work on, so I've actually been trying it with my yelling habit. My girls came with me on this trip, and when we are together in our room, it can get pretty tense. The tension I experienced in my own body when I tried to pause before yelling was very similar to what the others described."

"That's great, Jill. Thank you for sharing this with me. What you've experienced for yourself is another situation exposing the illusion that we have free will—how you, in this situation, experienced losing your control to something that made you act in a way you didn't want to. We're all victims of this mechanism more often than we realize, and this makes all aspects of our lives function less than optimally. In my book, I teach how this is connected to our Performance and Perfection Obsessed Culture and how to break free from it in the most essential areas of life by exposing and consciously confronting the tension and sensations we've been talking about. This is what will ultimately help people act more wisely and feel better about themselves and their lives. These benefits of training with the 3 Minute/3 Step Routine are experienced by people from all walks of life, no matter if they're highly challenged at the time or everything is already close to perfect for them."

Dr. Krinksted smiled encouragingly, and Jill seemed to take on a confidence she didn't have when she approached him. "Okay, so do you have any suggestions on how I can train until our next meeting?"

"No, it sounds like you're doing great. Just keep using this as your way of training. And don't be too hard on yourself if you really never get to stop or pause. Or if all you end up being able to do is to notice the experience of feeling what happens in your body when this whole thing plays out."

The doctor smiled again. "If you feel comfortable sharing this with the group, Jill, that would be great. I think the others would really benefit from your story. But please don't feel that you have to for any reason. The purpose of everything I teach is to help people break free from the societal pressure we're constantly under. Please only share this if you really feel like it at some point. Remember, we're here to break free from our Performance and Perfection Obsessed Culture, not add to it."

What Dr. Krinksted said made Jill feel really good inside. "Okay, thanks a lot for taking time to explain this, Dr. K. I'm divorced, and the girls are starting to say they want to live with their dad because he doesn't yell at them all the time. I know they're just saying that, but I think it really shows the impact my yelling has on them, so this is very important to me."

"Of course, I understand. Just keep practicing the 3/3 Routine, Jill. I promise it's going to make a huge difference in your life. See you this afternoon."

The Third Session

"They told me at the front desk that we are definitely going to be able to leave tomorrow, probably late morning," said Rohan to those who had arrived early.

"Yes, I heard that too," said Elinor. "I must say the last couple of days have been less of a strain since we've had Dr. K's program to look forward to, but it will still be good to get home."

There were murmurs of agreement, as the group assembled a few at a time. Dr. Krinksted was last to arrive. He took out his piece of paper with his notes. "I take it you've all heard we can go home tomorrow?" he asked.

"Yes," said Melanie. "In one way I'm glad, of course, but I was just getting into this course. Do you think there's any way we can continue after we all leave?"

"Yes, there is," said Dr. Krinksted, "but let's talk about that at the end of this session. In the meantime, I'm eager to hear about your experiences and learnings since yesterday. Who'll start off?"

"I will," said Cliff. "I really thought that I smoked because I loved it, and my joy in life would decrease if I quit. But from doing your 3/3 Routine, it's become obvious the real reason I smoke is the uncomfortable feeling I never noticed before when I am reaching for a cigarette."

"Yes, there's nothing better to soothe tension and discomfort in our bodies than all the typical things that we can become addicted to or overuse. Like food, sugar, nicotine, alcohol, sex, gambling, and all the other things that can end up as bad habits. I have never met a human being that didn't have at least one habit they had a hard time controlling because it soothed some tension or uncomfortable sensation in their body, a sensation they would like to change or numb. Sometimes I think we should redefine addiction because, in this sense, we are all addicts. We're not injecting heroin, but we all have some substance or action that reduces tension or uncomfortable sensations in our bodies that we haven't learned to tolerate."

Bad habits are not driven by the pleasure they provide, but by their role in reducing tension.

Dr. Krinksted realized he was on a roll again and was glad when Cliff interrupted him.

"When I got the message yesterday that we would have to wait until tomorrow instead of leaving today, I immediately felt like reaching for a cigarette. But because of what you have taught us, Doc, right away I became conscious of how the tension in my body had increased with the news, and I realized I wanted the cigarette so the tension would go away. So, when I took the cigarette, I was fully aware of what was happening, and I honestly felt I had a real choice about taking one or not, which I didn't feel I had before. And as I inhaled the smoke, I was aware of the physical response in my body that created the urge for the cigarette in the first place."

"That's great, Cliff, it's a real game changer when we realize that bad habits are not driven by the pleasure they provide, but by their role in reducing tension. Can you tell us a bit more about how all this made you feel?"

Cliff gazed into the distance, thinking before he spoke again, "Well, I must admit that when you first asked us to start looking for and observing what was happening in our bodies, I had no idea what you were talking about or what to look for. But when I began doing your 3 Minute/3 Step Routine, I did feel different things and began to recognize them. I've tried so many ways to quit smoking, and I thought this would be just another of the same. But it's not! I really get how your method is different. When I let go of trying to beat my bad habit using my willpower, I can experience your point. It's like as soon as I make it a willpower game, it's really hard to actually experience anything. I'm hooked, Dr. K—can't wait to see how this can help me in more areas of my life."

Melanie turned to her father and patted him on the shoulder. "Way to go, Dad! I felt a similar experience around chocolate as you did with cigarettes."

"Thank you for sharing your experience. And Cliff, your observation about how struggling to overcome your bad habit by using willpower makes it harder to experience is correct. In fact, it's much more important than you can imagine. We'll get back to it later because it's closely related to how our unhealthy culture damages our lives. Does anyone else have anything to share?"

After a moment, Diana, the redheaded solo traveler who always sat at the end of a row, spoke up, "I wish I could tell a similar story, but I can't. I don't know why, but I haven't really been able to apply your 3/3 method at all, and I'm curious as to why that is."

"Okay, Diana," said Dr. Krinksted. "Would it be okay for you to tell us the habit you've been working on and what you have been experiencing?"

"It's hard to explain, but I'm working on relaxing and doing nothing. Sounds so simple, but I just can't do it. Never have. When I try to sit still and relax, there's a restlessness in my body that takes over. It feels intolerable, to use your word, Dr. K, and I just have to get up and do something—anything!"

"From what you've said, you have actually identified what is happening in your body—a physical sensation in the form of what you call restlessness. Very often, it's almost impossible to truly grasp or describe these physical sensations when we first expose them, so how you experience this make total sense, Diana. Have you ever been aware of this restlessness before?"

Diana's face suddenly lit up, and she smiled. "No, I haven't," she said. "I only noticed it since I began to try your 3/3 Routine."

If there were no cravings, there would be no bad habits.

"Well, there you are, then. To me, it sounds like you are becoming aware of something happening in your body that you haven't noticed before; it's just different from what you thought it should be."

Diana nodded.

"It's not a coincidence that I use the word *intolerable* for this sensation you're all becoming aware of, Diana. It's because it's intolerable that we end up giving in to things we know are not in our best interest or in anybody's best interest, really. Not acting *wisely* as I've come to call it. If the feeling didn't seem intolerable, the connection to the rational parts of our brains would stay intact, and we wouldn't end up acting against our own will, so to speak."

"So, is that what we call cravings?" asked Harini.

"Exactly, Harini," replied Dr. Krinksted. "All bad habits are connected to some tension or uncomfortable sensations in our bodies that we would like to change or make go away. This is what we call cravings. If there were no tension or uncomfortable sensations that were hard for us to tolerate, we simply wouldn't indulge in the bad habit! If there were no cravings, there would be no bad habits. Period. That's the short version of how and why the 3/3 Routine works so well on our bad habits. When you expose and consciously confront the tension and uncomfortable sensations that we call cravings, you will become able to tolerate it better because you're teaching your nervous system that these sensations aren't dangerous. So, you won't have to use your bad habit—your drug as I call it—to change them or make them go away."

He stopped talking, giving the group a few moments to digest what he'd told them. Some were nodding thoughtfully; others looked as if they'd suddenly gotten it. "Diana," he continued, "could you try to describe how you experience this intolerable sensation that makes you want to get up and do something?"

"I'm not sure I can, to tell you the truth. I just know I can't stand it. It's almost like I can't be in my body—that probably sounds crazy, I know."

"No, it doesn't sound crazy at all. I'm sure looking back we've all experienced the results of our version of an intolerable sensation even though we weren't aware of it at the time—and ended up doing something that made us feel stupid. It's all about that unpleasant tension or sensation we're talking about. And just to remind you, the physical discomfort I keep referring to will be different for each of you, so don't worry if what you experience seems different from how it feels for someone else. The important thing is that you start becoming aware of it when it's there."

"So, what you're saying is that from the smallest bad habit to bad habits that have more severe consequences, it all comes back to that discomfort in my body that I haven't confronted and learned to tolerate?" Harini asked for clarification.

"Exactly. For example, when a smoker becomes able to tolerate the tension and sensations of their cravings for nicotine, they will just quit if that's what they want. When a person who feels they have a weight problem becomes able to tolerate the tension and sensations of their cravings for food, they will just start eating less or less often. I continue using these examples, but this goes for all bad habits; it's the same mechanism.

"But as I've said before, this tension and these uncomfortable sensations have a wide spectrum of intensity—from just a vague tension at one end to unbearable at the other—so it's simple but not necessarily easy, as some of you have already experienced. Sometimes this intolerable sensation can feel like strong emotions, such as sadness, anxiety, or loneliness. But we rarely let it go that far before taking the action or substance that reduces the discomfort. Maybe you've heard the term *mood-changing substances or activities*. To some extent, all bad habits are mood-changing substances or activities because changing these sensations in our bodies is intimately connected to changing our mood. Bad habits and acting unwisely are so much more than eating a whole tub of ice cream, or spending money on something we don't need and really can't afford, or having sex with someone we really shouldn't."

The doctor's last comment caused a ripple in the group, a mix of chuckles and puzzled frowns. Clearly the group was finding a wider understanding of the implications of the illusion of free will and the potential power of the 3 Minute/3 Step Routine.

"So, getting back to you, Diana," he said. "You're already on the right track with what's happening to you during the 3/3 Routine. You just need to keep experiencing it all in the moment, recognizing what it feels like to you, and experiencing how the intolerable discomfort makes you give in almost at once. Are you ever able to relax?"

"No, not really. I usually have a drink or two when I get home from work to relax. I'm not an alcoholic, but I feel that my before-dinner drinks help me let go of all the work problems at the end of the day."

"Yes, for many people, alcohol is an effective but not necessarily wise way of soothing stress and discomfort. So, when do you typically have a drink?"

"When I come home from work, as I've said. And usually another one after dinner."

"Okay then, besides observing the tension and sensations in your body as you try to relax, you might also try the 3 Minute/3 Step Routine when you're about to have a drink. I promise you'll slowly be able to better tolerate the discomfort that seems unbearable right now. Will you try that?"

"Sure. I'd love to be able to relax without having to take a drink. It would be nice to be more in control and to have a drink when I feel like it, rather than depending on it to relax."

There's a big difference between healthy use, overuse or abuse, and actual addiction.

"Yes, feeling we have true freedom of choice is what we all want so that we can enjoy actions and substances that make us feel good without the risk of abuse or becoming addicted. Melanie, I'm sure you'd love to have the odd piece of chocolate once in a while without ending up eating the whole bar, yes?"

"Oh yes, definitely!" said Melanie. "I'd hate to have to give it up altogether just to make sure not to fall into the bad habit part of it again and again."

"Yes, there's a big difference between healthy use, overuse or abuse, and actual addiction. If I get the chance, I'll talk more about that later. Any more questions or experiences to share?"

"Actually, I had kind of a strange experience yesterday," said Rohan. "I have a bad habit of looking at my phone all the time, which annoys some people. When the internet went off the other day, I thought I would have a really hard time not being able to check my phone, but the funny thing is—I didn't really miss it. I quite enjoyed being more present. But as soon as the internet came back yesterday, I couldn't help but start looking at my phone again. Kind of strange since I actually enjoyed being without it.

"Just for fun, I started using your 3/3 Routine on this to see what would happen, and I had a similar experience to what some of you have described. I never really thought of my constant phone checking as a bad habit, as it didn't seem to me like something I was craving, but I have to admit that I do it more than I really want to. I'm curious though, Dr. K—is this driven by the same mechanism?"

"Yes, it's interesting that you recognized that, Rohan, because it means you are really getting what I mean when I talk about the illusion of free will.

"The mechanism behind this is pretty much the same as what we usually see as bad habits. Maybe some of you remember that I used this as one of the examples of how to phrase your bad habit the first day we met. It's the same kind of tension or sensation in your body that gives you the impulse to pick up your phone and look at it, and when doing so, the tension or sensation changes or goes away. Just like any other bad habit we've talked about. So, when the discomfort starts in your body, and your nervous system subconsciously knows that picking up your phone will make the feeling more tolerable or make it go away completely, it puts the thought into your head and makes you do it. And just as with all the other bad habits, this will change when you regularly expose, and consciously confront, the tension and uncomfortable sensations in your body related to your urge to pick up your phone."

"Yes," said Rohan, "I can totally see that now. Funny how I was never aware of it before." Rohan looked at his wife. "I know the phone thing bothers you, honey, so let's hope I can work on it with the 3/3 Routine."

Harini smiled and squeezed her husband's hand.

"The fact is," said Dr. Krinksted, "every time you make a wise decision not to do something and end up doing it anyway, it's this mechanism at play. You are being controlled by tension or sensations your nervous system acts on while you might not even be consciously aware of it.

"It can be hard to grasp, which is why we started at the light end of the spectrum by focusing on what we call bad habits because it's the easiest way to give someone the experience of this. It's also the low-hanging fruit for experiencing your first benefit of the 3 Minute/3 Step Routine. But let's move on now and talk about how all this relates to how our Performance and Perfection Obsessed Culture creates all these self-inflicted problems and prevents us from experiencing true fulfilment."

"Excuse me, Dr. K," said Melanie, raising her hand.

"Yes, Melanie?"

"What do you mean by self-inflicted?"

"Well, there are some problems in life we just can't control. No matter how much we're told that we should enjoy every minute of our lives, the truth is that life can be tough. I know we generally don't have a problem getting food and water like in some parts of the world, but there are still problems beyond our control. On top of all the existential challenges every human being faces, like losing our health or our loved ones, we can lose our jobs because the company goes out of business and things like that.

"But we are also guilty of worrying unnecessarily about things that are not really that important, what we sometimes jokingly call *first-world problems*.

"I call them self-inflicted when they are rooted in our cultural beliefs—being so performance and perfection obsessed—feeling that no matter how much we are or do, it's never enough. Please understand, though, that I'm not saying that making these situations into big problems are people's own fault. Not at all. We are simply victims of the culture we grow up in and live in. Do you understand the distinction I'm making?"

"What I'm hearing, Doc," said Cliff, "is that it's the fault of our culture, but it's still something that each of us can affect if we know how. For example, by training your 3/3 Routine. Is that right?"

What's ingrained in us by our culture makes it almost impossible to feel truly fulfilled.

"Exactly, Cliff. And I'm also saying that if enough people do this, it will also change the culture in the long-term—in fact, that's one of the reasons I'm so passionate about getting this out to the world. It just isn't fair that what's ingrained in us by our culture—and what we keep ingraining in each other and in our kids and youth—makes us feel bad about ourselves and our lives and makes it almost impossible to feel truly fulfilled.

"This makes me want to say a little more about fault and blame. None of this is really your fault. If we had free will, it could be. But as you know by now, that's a myth. We're not in charge of our nervous system; it's our nervous system that's in charge of us. If we want to talk about being weak, weak is normal because of this deeply rooted mechanism in our nervous systems that makes us weak. Until we really understand these facts, we'll keep blaming ourselves for being stupid or weak and keep feeling inadequate and unsuccessful."

"So, all this is going to change when we incorporate your 3/3 method in our lives?" asked Alex, sounding a bit like his old skeptical self.

"Exactly, Alex. Even though you may still doubt it, when you regularly train and use your ability to expose and consciously confront all the uncomfortable tension and sensations in your body, you will keep the connection to the rational parts of your brain more open in more and more situations, and you'll start acting more wisely in all areas and aspects of your life without even having to try hard. Does that sound good to everyone?"

Alex grunted. "It does, but I still think it sounds too good to be true."

Dr. Krinksted smiled, having heard that many times. "I understand, Alex, I really do. And please bear with me and let me prove you wrong. So having said that, we're ready to move on to the next level. It's time to look at how you can use the 3 Minute/3 Step Routine to reduce unnecessary stress and worry."

CHAPTER 4

How to Reduce Unnecessary Stress and Worry

Without Lowering Your Standards

"I think we can all agree that the situation we find ourselves in right now—being stuck on this island—is stressful."
Nods all around and some exclamations proclaimed everyone's agreement.

"So, our situation is a good opportunity to work on our next topic on how using the 3 Minute/3 Step Routine will reduce what I call the unnecessary part of your stress and worrying. Are you ready for this?"

"Oh yes! This one has my name written all over it," said Jill loudly, which brought a few laughs and nods of agreement.

"Okay, what we're doing now is upping the ante on the training. Up to now, you've been training with the 3 Minute/3 Step Routine in specific situations where you had complete control over how much discomfort you were willing to put up with. You could end the routine and discomfort at any time by giving in to your bad habit and ending the craving.

"When it comes to stress and worrying though, it's more difficult for most people—but it's also upping the ante on the benefits you'll experience from the training.

"You'll remember how you learned that the root cause of your bad habits is not what you thought it was. It wasn't about the pleasure it gave you; you actually indulge in these habits to relieve discomfort in your body. You're about to find out that it's exactly the same when it comes to stress and worrying —the root cause isn't what you've learned!

What stresses and worries you isn't really about the outside circumstances; it's about how your nervous system interprets them.

"The fact is that what stresses and worries you isn't really about the outside circumstances; it's about how your nervous system *interprets* them. Consider the example we talked about before, being afraid of spiders. If your nervous system interprets the presence of a spider as dangerous, then when you see one, tension and uncomfortable sensations develop in you. The connection to the rational parts of your brain is temporarily cut off to some extent, making the more primitive parts of your brain take over, so you react more instinctively. This makes you able to act more quickly, but also more irrationally in this situation, given that the spider really isn't dangerous at all. If it wasn't for this misinterpretation, you would keep the connection to the rational parts of your brain fully open, letting you have a real choice about how to act wisely: remove it, or just let the spider do its thing like it would if you hadn't even seen it in the first place."

Dr. Krinksted took a short pause.

"It's the same way the societal pressure in our Performance and Perfection Obsessed Culture makes us act irrationally. It's ingrained in us that if we're not superhuman—being perfect and able to over-perform again and again in all areas of our lives all the time—every time we aren't and can't, our nervous system interprets this as danger. This happens regularly for most of us because none of us are superhuman. And what happens? Yes, the connection to the rational parts of our brains shuts off so it's impossible for us to act wisely. Nobody can change our unhealthy culture from one day to the next, but what we can do from one day to the next is start exposing and confronting the discomfort in our bodies created by all this societal pressure that holds us hostage. Increasing our ability to tolerate discomfort in our bodies will change the whole picture for stress and worry, just like it does regarding bad habits. We cannot change how our nervous system is wired, but we can change the misinterpretation of danger so that the normal wiring of our nervous system doesn't make us act irrationally. The best part is you'll be able to change your level of stress and worrying without necessarily needing to take on less work or things that are important to you. Again, it's about creating a situation where you have the freedom to act wisely—giving you what you want—instead of what your nervous system is forcing you to do out of fear."

"Sorry to interrupt, Dr. K," said Laura. "But a lot of people talk about how our nervous system is not made for the modern life of the twenty-first century, that it's our nervous system that's at fault. Are you saying that that's not true, that there's nothing wrong with our nervous systems? And that it's only our Performance and Perfection Obsessed Culture that's the villain? And that your simple 3/3 Routine works not only on bad habits, but will also help me reduce my stress level?"

"That's a lot of questions, Laura . . . and yes, that's exactly right. I'll come back to this next time we meet, but there's absolutely nothing wrong with the human nervous system. It's as perfect as can be. It reacts when perceiving danger exactly the way it's supposed to. If it didn't, we would be in more trouble. The real villain is our unhealthy culture that ingrains in us that things that are perfectly normal for a normal human being are dangerous: like making mistakes, like not being able to live up to everybody's expectations all the time, like not looking or being perfect, like not being productive, effective, and happy 24/7. I could go on and on. Being just human instead of superhuman as I call it. That's the villain, not our nervous system. And that's the great news, because you can't change your nervous system, but you can learn to break free from the unhealthy norms and rules in our culture. And after getting acquainted with the 3 Minute/3 Step Routine by using it to overcome your bad habits, the next step is using the exact same routine to help you reduce the unnecessary part of your stress and worrying.

"What you're going to find as you keep practicing the 3/3 Routine is that the root cause of not only bad habits but also much of your stress and worry is your nervous system's interpretation and misinterpretation of the tension and sensations that a specific situation creates in your body. Not the specific situation itself. And to be able to act more wisely in regard to stress and worry, you also need to consciously expose the tension and uncomfortable sensations and force your nervous system to have a second look at its interpretations in these situations. This is part of what's happening every time you do the 3 Minute/3 Step Routine.

"I'm looking forward to discussing this in more depth after you've had a go at expanding the training to include such situations. Here's what that will look like."

Dr. Krinksted handed out a piece of paper with the 3 Minute/3 Step Routine they were going to use in regards to this new topic.

The 3 Minute/3 Step Routine for Reducing Unnecessary Stress and Worry

Step 1: Stop and observe

Like the 3/3 Routine regarding a bad habit, when using the 3/3 in regard to unnecessary stress and worry, the first step is to stop and observe. But at this stage of your training, on top of observing the tension and sensations in your body, I want you to observe what is happening in your mind.

So, every time you find yourself feeling stressed or worried or in front of a decision that might affect your stress level, I want you to stop in that moment, take a deep breath through your nose, and observe the thoughts that run through your mind as well as what happens in your body.

Step 2: Pause and observe

While you pause for as long as you like, note how the tension or uncomfortable sensations you observed in your body in step 1 might be building up in strength, or if new tension or uncomfortable sensations are emerging in your body. Also keep observing the thoughts that run through your mind.

Remember that the 3 Minute/3 Step Routine is not a training of your willpower; it's a training of your ability to observe. So, pause as long as you like while observing what is happening in your body and in your mind without trying to change anything.

And again, while you pause, don't hesitate to take some deep breaths as this will help you in your endeavor.

Step 3: Continue and observe

When you don't feel like pausing any longer, observe the tension and sensations in your body and the thoughts running through your mind as you continue your activity where you left off before starting this specific 3/3 Routine.

"Is that clear to everyone?"

"Yes, although it is a bit different from the bad habit routine, as you said," said Jill. "But I'll definitely give it a try."

"Great," the doctor replied. "Also, it appears that one source of our collective stress is about to be lifted. I understand it's definite that we can leave around noon tomorrow. So, I have a question for you all: Would you like to continue with the training, and if so, would you be open to doing virtual calls from wherever you live?"

Melanie spontaneously jumped to her feet, clapping her hands. "Oh yes!" she exclaimed. "I was going to suggest that myself, but you've beaten me to it."

"Great idea," said Elinor, "count me in."

One by one, everyone said they'd like to continue virtually—even Alex, which surprised and pleased Dr. Krinksted.

"All right. I'd like you all to write your email addresses on a piece of paper now and hand it to me before you leave. I will send you the link before each meeting. What would you say to having our first meeting next Friday at the same time? You'll have to work out the local time wherever you live, of course."

There was a little discussion, but in the end, they all said yes.

"Okay then," said Dr. Krinksted, gathering up his things. "Have a safe trip home everybody, and I'll see you all next week!"

The First Virtual Meeting

On the plane back from the island, Dr. Krinksted had made additions about the participants in his notes. Before opening the meeting, he put the updated sheet in front of his screen and reviewed it.

Notes:

Melanie, Melanie's mother, Irene, and Melanie's father, Cliff

Melanie

Thirty-one years old.

The enthusiastic young woman who reached out to me and initiated our group meeting. Bought the book because she wants to break a bad habit.

But also wants to better understand how our Performance and Perfection Obsessed Culture messes up her life and how she can break away from it more. Likes that it's all based on neuroscience.

Bad habit: Has a sweet tooth.

Has started recognizing different sensations related to her cravings for sweets.

Irene, Melanie's mother

Showed up to support her daughter. She is a physician, and she wants to make sure what her daughter is into is something sound and rational. As a physician, she's also open to learning something new that might allow her to better help the stressed patients in her clinic.

Nothing new.

Cliff, Melanie's father

Told us that his daughter, Melanie, talked him into joining.

Bad habit: Smoking.

Has tried to quit many times but never succeeded. This is what he's using the 3/3 Routine to work on.

Has already experienced that beating his bad habit using the 3/3 Routine instead of trying to use his willpower works in a totally different manner. Has really started to gain a whole new experience of all the tension and thoughts related to his bad habit of smoking (his craving for nicotine) via the 3/3 Routine. It has become obvious to him that the real reason he smokes is not the pleasure it gives him but the tension and uncomfortable sensations he never noticed before when he reaches out for a cigarette—and how his urge for a cigarette increases in strength when this tension and sensations increase.

He's also catching on to how our Performance and Perfection Obsessed Culture is a real villain in our lives but still something that each of us can break free from when we learn how.

Told us that he can't wait to see how this will help him in more areas of his life when we get to that.

Alex and Barbara

They are probably in their forties.

Alex

The guy I heard complaining at the reception desk. He said he showed up because he didn't have anything better to do. He generally seems to have a bad temper and he's very skeptical. He was the one who almost left when I mentioned the notion that free will is an illusion. I think he might be more stressed than he is aware of, and I got the impression that he's not very open to trying to see things in a new way no matter how true or wise it is.

Nothing new.

Barbara

Didn't say much. Seemed embarrassed by Alex's temper and behavior.

Nothing new.

Rohan and Harini

They are here with their young daughter.

Rohan

The guy I saw sitting in the lobby flirting with a woman when his wife and daughter entered. He did the introduction of his wife.

Bad habit: Checking his inbox all the time.

Told us of another bad habit—constant phone checking—uses the 3/3 Routine for this.

Harini

Didn't say much.

Bad habit: Nail biting. Told us that she hates herself for—and is embarrassed by—her lack of self-control.

Has started noticing something new when doing the 3/3 Routine, but hasn't yet exposed exactly what the tension and uncomfortable sensations related to her nail biting are in her.

Seems interested in learning more.

Diana

The red-haired woman who was the object of Rohan's attentions in the lobby. She is travelling by herself.

Mentioned her inability to relax. The 3/3 Routine has made her aware of the tension and sensations that are connected to this. She uses alcohol to relax and will start using the 3/3 Routine to gain more control of this.

Elinor and Phil

The stylish, blond woman and the man that I saw in the dining area that had the discussion about her shopping and his eating habits.

They have a six-year-old girl and a twelve-year-old boy.

At the meeting, I felt tension between them.

Elinor

Introduced both of them.

Seems like she already likes my teachings and the 3/3 Routine.

Phil

Said that Elinor dragged him along to our meeting.

Seems to have caught interest in what I'm teaching. He mentioned that he's using the 3/3 when the urge for reaching for a bag of potato chips or a second burger shows up.

Laura and Hannah

The young couple.

Laura

The inquisitive one who was doing a master's in psychology.

Has a strong professional interest in everything I teach.

Hannah

Didn't say much. Was introduced by her fiancée, Laura.

Still hasn't shared or asked anything.

Jill

The woman who asked the question about being triggered when her two young daughters tease each other. She's alone with them here on vacation.

It was Jill I had the private talk with. Uses the 3/3 Routine when being triggered when her two young daughters tease each other.

When starting the topic on unnecessary stress and worry, she said that her name was written all over that topic.

Yan

The oldest guy who sat in the back. Didn't share anything yet.

Still hasn't shared or asked anything yet.

Dr. Krinksted clicked the start button, and the screen gradually filled up as everyone logged into the meeting. He welcomed them. "Hello again, everyone! I'm glad you all decided to join me virtually to continue your training in more and more important areas and aspects of your life. How have things been generally over the past week since you left the island?"

"What a relief to get home!" said Elinor. "I love going on vacation, but luckily, I always love coming back home as well—especially this time where we ended up being away longer than planned without having any say in it."

"You can say that again," agreed Diana. "When I got home, I sat on my couch for half an hour, just appreciating being in my own apartment."

"Yeah, but all the stress from work came back with it," said Alex. "A lot of work had piled up for me during the vacation."

"Interesting, Alex," said Dr. Krinksted. "Were you able to use any of the training I introduced at our last session on the island to deal with the situation?"

Alex nodded. "You know, Dr. K, that's what has convinced me more than anything else that what you're teaching us really works. When I arrived in the office, I was anxious to get to my desk and find out what had accumulated, but everybody wanted to hear about what happened on the island, and I felt I had to spend time answering their questions. I couldn't really do your 3/3 Routine at that time because, of course, we were talking, so by the time I got to my desk, I noticed I felt really tense. So, I stopped and went through your routine before opening my computer.

"In the first step, after taking a deep breath, I realized that the uncomfortable sensation felt like what we usually call a knot in the stomach. I took a moment and just experienced it. Then, even though I was itching to log into my system, I paused. I sat in my chair for three full minutes, experiencing the tension grow more and more intense—it was almost like I could imagine the knot getting bigger and bigger. Not a nice feeling at all.

"When I finally gave in and switched on my computer, I felt the tension diminishing. But when I started seeing the emails and the reports from my staff and realized just how much more work I had to do, it started building up again."

Dr. Krinksted nodded and gave a little sympathetic smile, having experienced something similar again and again in his own life. "Yes, that doesn't surprise me, Alex."

"But something else happened. I noticed my mind seemed to go berserk worrying about how I was going to get it all done. I'm not great at delegating work to other people; I guess I worry that tasks might end up not being done, or not done as well as I would do it myself. But this time, I simply confronted this tension I felt in my stomach when thinking about delegating some of the tasks that other people would be able to do just as well, which I knew would be the wise thing to do. I had a staff meeting and delegated a lot of it, more than I normally would. It wasn't easy. I felt tension in my body throughout the whole process and a little voice telling me how this could go all wrong. But I was able to confront this tension and do it anyway. I still had a lot to do, but it was more manageable, and the tasks I kept were the kind that really belonged to me. The tension got so low that for most of the rest of the day, I almost didn't notice it."

This was an Alex that none of them had seen before. He told his story enthusiastically, with none of his usual gruff complaining.

His wife, Barbara, was sitting next to him in front of the same camera. She had a little smile on her face as she listened.

"Congratulations, Alex!" said Rohan. "What a great result, man."

"Yes, this is a great example of what can happen when we give our nervous system a new opportunity to experience if a circumstance leads to real danger or not," the doctor added. "Who else has something to share?"

"I'll tell you, Dr. K," said Phil. "It's been an eye opener to me how often I have tension in my body that I haven't been aware of before. The more I paid attention, the more I realized how the level of discomfort continually goes up and down, affecting my feelings of control."

"Can you be more specific?"

"Yes, as I've indicated before, the bad habit I chose to work on was my eating habits. I simply eat too much and too often, something I know isn't really good for me. And with this deeper level of using your method, I began to realize it's more complex than a simple habit.

"Yesterday, I began to feel hungry just before noon, but I couldn't leave the shop at that time to go to the burger place down the street. Because of what I've learned from you, instead of just feeling more and more hungry, I was able to observe the feeling I usually call *being hungry*. I was able to watch the tension and sensations you've talked about building up in me. It never actually became intolerable, but I realized that not being able to get the lunch I wanted was causing stress on top of the uncomfortable feeling of being hungry."

Dr. Krinksted nodded. "Thanks for sharing that, Phil."

But Phil wasn't finished yet. "Can I just tell you something else, Dr. K?"

"Of course."

"Any of my staff will tell you I can be a bit of a bear at work and easily lose my temper with them. By using your 3/3 Routine on this problem, I clearly saw that it was that tension building to the point where I had a hard time standing it. And if I wasn't able to eat, I felt like taking it out on them to relieve some tension. I'm working on that now as a separate aspect of my problem, and I can see it's beginning to work."

Phil laughed before continuing. "If I succeed with both of these things, I'll soon be this slim and balanced guy that my staff won't recognize!"

Everyone laughed at this new image of Phil, and his wife shook her head with a smile. Clearly, the training was paying off for Phil.

"Anyone else have an experience or insight around stress and worrying?"

Barbara, Alex's wife, who was usually very quiet at the sessions, sat forward a little and seemed to be gathering her courage. "Yes, I do, Dr. K," she said. She looked a little nervously at her husband, who seemed surprised. "I know I'm the worrying type, but practicing this routine over the past weeks has made me realize how often I worry— which seems to be practically all the time. What are people thinking of me? Are my kids okay? Can we pay our mortgage if interest rates go up? And that's just the small stuff."

"What do you mean, *the small stuff*? This sounds rather profound to me."

"Well, it's hard for me to talk about this out loud, especially as I haven't spoken to Alex about it first, but I realize now how often I feel that discomfort building up in my body when Alex behaves in certain ways. I'm very aware of how he behaves and reacts and also what I might have done wrong to provoke him."

Alex was also sitting forward now, a little frown on his face, listening attentively. Dr. Krinksted had the feeling that listening to his wife talk this way was a new experience for them both.

"Just yesterday evening he went for a walk by himself, and because of this training, I noticed tension immediately started building up in me. I worried about what I might have done that had upset him, or if I hadn't done something he wanted me to do."

"But Barbara," interrupted Alex, "I just wanted to be alone to figure out a problem at work. It had nothing to do with you!"

"That's good to know, Alex, but I'm just trying to explain how I felt. As the discomfort built up in my body, I noticed my thoughts went out of control. I even noticed that I began to wonder what would happen if Alex wanted a divorce."

"Barbara . . ."

Dr. Krinksted held up his hand for Alex to stop. "Please let her finish, Alex. It's important for her to speak up, and she is sharing an experience that could be valuable for everybody to hear."

"I thought about how bad that would be for the kids. Then that made me wonder if I was a good enough mother: Would my kids grow up to be happy? From there, I noticed how my thoughts jumped to my job, and I worried whether I was living up to my boss's expectations and if I was risking getting fired. It just went from bad to worse, and the tension in my body felt as if I was going to explode. I sometimes wonder if I'm going crazy, Dr. K."

"No, you're not crazy, Barbara," the doctor reassured her with a gentle smile. "The fact is our nervous systems are subconsciously scanning our environment all the time for situations that it interprets—or misinterprets—as dangerous in the pursuit of making us thrive and survive. I'm not sure if any of you noticed this, but Barbara started talking about worrying, rather than stress, as if they were the same thing. They're really not, but it's natural to make this assumption because they are connected in much the same way as cravings and bad habits. Just as having cravings can lead to bad habits, it's the worrying that leads to stress."

Alex spoke up, an expression of understanding on his face, "I know exactly what you mean, Dr. K. It's so obvious to me now that when I'm worried, I often end up acting in a way that doesn't serve me and that leads to even more stress. It makes the sensations in my body even harder to deal with."

"Yes, it really is a vicious circle."

Alex turned to Barbara, "Honey, I had no idea you were feeling like this, that my behavior put stress on you like this."

Barbara smiled a little. "Well, we never talk about these things, Alex, and now I know the reason why. It's because I'm afraid to rock the boat even more. Maybe Dr. K's training has highlighted our need to work on our communication on top of helping us being able to actually do it."

The whole group seemed to be empathizing with the couple in this emotional moment.

Then Laura spoke up. "Not sure I'm getting this, Dr. K," said Laura. "You said that after we'd experienced this for ourselves, you would give us some more background information. Could you do that now?"

"Yes, this is perfect timing, Laura. Okay, so what exactly is worry?" the doctor began with a rhetorical question. "We usually understand it as thoughts about how to avoid something we consider bad from happening in the future. This might include getting hurt or being divorced. It also might be about something we're afraid of *not* happening, like not getting a job we want, or things like that. But as usual, we're missing the root cause here. What we're really trying to prevent is not the event itself, but the hard-to-tolerate tension and sensations that our nervous system knows will be created if the thing we interpret as *bad* happens or the thing we interpret as *good* doesn't happen. On top of this, these so-called good or bad things aren't even truly good or bad a lot of the time because that definition is dictated by our villain, the Performance and Perfection Obsessed Culture.

"And just like your experience of working with cravings using the 3 Minute/3 Step Routine eventually stops your reliance on bad habits, so will being able to tolerate the tension we call worrying eventually stop the unnecessary part of worrying. Again, what you have to do is develop your ability to tolerate any and all sensations that might arise in your body. How do you think you will do that?"

"By consciously exposing and confronting them directly using your 3/3 Routine," replied Melanie and her father in unison, making everyone laugh. Melanie and Cliff gave each other a virtual high-five, and Irene looked on fondly.

"Exactly!" said Dr. Krinksted, laughing too. "I love how you're getting this! When your nervous system learns from experience that no matter what happens on the outside, you'll be able to confront and tolerate the resulting tension and sensations inside your body, your nervous system will stop having to think through all possible scenarios again and again to avoid something specific happening or working to make something specific happen. And here's my question to you: What's another word for thinking through all possible scenarios again and again to avoid something from happening?"

"Worrying!" said Rohan.

"Exactly, Rohan. And what will you experience instead by increasing your ability to tolerate all the tension and uncomfortable sensations in your body?"

"Peace of mind I would call it, literally speaking."

"Exactly—or at least more peace of mind. I add that caveat because we are all just human, and worrying is another totally normal part of our human nature. Our human nervous system's ability to analyze and try to predict and control outcomes is one of our most important abilities; it's what has enabled us to thrive and survive as a species better than any other creatures on this planet. It's one of the reasons there's eight billion of us, and we've become rulers of the world. So, we'll never be able to stop worrying altogether, and that's a good thing, because that would stop us from being able to avoid real danger."

"Ah, that makes sense, so it's the *unnecessary* worrying that will stop?" Laura noted.

"Yes, it's the worrying about things that aren't likely to happen— or that wouldn't be objectively very dangerous if they did—that will decrease. It's the compulsive part of worrying, the *overthinking* as some people call it. In the same way, it's the compulsive part of an action or a habit that makes it a bad habit—when it goes from wise use to unwise abuse or addiction. That's why we can deal with it in the same way."

"I like that," said Alex thoughtfully. "But some of the things I worry about are outside my control, Dr. K. How does that fit into your scenario?"

"Well, let me ask you, Alex. If you had true freedom of choice in the matter, what would you like to do? What would be the wise thing to do?"

Alex thought for a moment before answering. "Well, I think it would be good to think about the result I want, do whatever I can to make that happen, and then let it go, knowing that I had done everything I could—and stop worrying."

"Right, and that's what will end up happening automatically more often when you do this training. When your nervous system learns from experience that it can tolerate most of the bodily tension that outside situations can induce in you, it doesn't have to meticulously think through any and all scenarios again and again. And it's not that it *wants* to experience the tension and uncomfortable sensations, just that it knows it *can* tolerate it. There's a world of difference between preferring not to experience discomfort and needing not to experience discomfort. Can you see the difference?"

"Yes, I think so," said Alex. "It does make sense. It's like the difference between needing something and wanting something; the difference in the amount of stress it causes is huge. I just hope it works."

"Me too," said Cliff. "It does sound a bit too good to be true, Dr. K. You know, if there was just one thing I could change in my life, this would be it—to be able to stress and worry less. I've already experienced cutting back on my smoking with your method, so I'm ready to give this a serious try."

Jill put her hand up to ask if she could change the subject. "I don't know why this is, but somehow over the last couple of days, I've felt more grounded. Does that make sense in the context of what you've been teaching us, Dr. K?"

"Jill, I can't tell you how pleased I am to hear you say that. You see, no matter how great it feels to solve your immediate challenges with bad habits, stress, and worry, this skill of consciously exposing and confronting the tension and uncomfortable sensations in our bodies will do so much more than that. In my view, it does something much more important and beneficial. What you call *being grounded* is a great way to describe one of the best benefits of persistently and consistently practicing the 3 Minute/3 Step Routine. For me, feeling grounded means feeling okay in my own skin with whatever tension and sensations I experience in any given situation.

"I've mentioned several times that the way we typically look at a lot of things in our culture is often inaccurate or wrong, and this goes for stress as well. Typically, we think of stress as just having too much on our plates, but the truth is having too much on our plates doesn't really cause stress unless we worry about it. It's the worry, not the workload, that causes the unnecessary part of stress that we don't like—and that can make us sick! But since a big workload and a lot of worry often go together, we typically don't realize this. Let me try to illustrate this for you.

"Let's say your garage has become so full of junk that you have no room to put your car. You know it's a big job to clear it out, but the fact is, it's been like that for months and there haven't really been any consequences. So, you don't worry about it, and, therefore, it doesn't cause you stress."

A couple of the group were looking as if they might question this, but Dr. Krinksted held up his hand before continuing.

"Let's move over now to a work example—in fact, let's look at Alex's example that he just gave us. When he got back from the island, there was a huge amount of work backed up for him, and his stress level immediately shot up. But I want to suggest that it wasn't the amount of work that caused the stress, but fear of the consequences for not getting it all done. Am I right, Alex?"

"Yes, right on the money, Dr. K. If some of those things fell down a crack, it could badly affect the results of some major projects we have going on. So, yes, I worried about that."

"So, fear of the consequences is the equivalent of what?"

"Worrying!"

"Right, Melanie! Now, if we don't see any negative consequences of having the garage full of junk, we don't worry—therefore, no stress. But what if we buy a new car? We don't want it sitting out in the driveway because there have been a lot of burglaries in the neighborhood lately, so every day it's out is a risk. We want it safe in the garage, but all that junk is in the way. Suddenly, we feel there might be consequences that would make us feel bad, you know, create tension in our bodies if the car was damaged because we hadn't made room for it in the garage. Now we're talking stress!"

Laura raised her hand slightly while starting to talk, "Dr. K, in your example, would it be the same if we were afraid what other people might think of us even before having the car challenge? You know, like you've mentioned numerous times, in our Performance and Perfection Obsessed Culture, leaving a mess in our garage and not keeping it tidy—couldn't that lead to the exact same thing, unnecessary stress and worry? Because of what kind of person we think we would look like?"

"Definitely, Laura. That's exactly how this invisible villain can and will affect us subconsciously all the time." The doctor showed his thumps up to Laura.

"You know," said Diana, "My brother-in-law is a busy lawyer who works long hours and always has a packed schedule, but he says he never feels stressed. I'm beginning to understand why. It's because he doesn't worry about it. In fact, he thrives on it, and that's why he's not stressed. That's fascinating, Dr. K."

"It also explains my Aunt Bessie," said Melanie, laughing. "She gets stressed just having a few guests over for dinner—she starts laying the table two days in advance."

"Yes," said Irene, laughing. "She's my sister, and what Melanie says is true. She's always been a worrier and is always stressed out."

"But," said Dr. Krinksted, "starting her preparations so far in advance might simply be her way of reducing the unnecessary stress she would otherwise feel the days before she has guests. What we don't know is if she feels she really has a choice in regard to acting this way—if it's a problem for her or just her healthy way of coping. See, it's all about how our nervous system interprets what's going on."

"True. I never thought of that," said Irene.

"There's another factor in all this," said the doctor. "Let's come back to a personal example here. Jill, you have kids. Have you ever found yourself agreeing to do something for their school even though you didn't really feel you had the time and energy for it?"

"Oh yes, that happens regularly."

"Why do you think that is?"

Jill thought for a moment before answering, "Well, I guess it's because I want the teachers or other parents to like me and not think badly of me."

"In other words, because you want to live up to societal expectations?"

Jill nodded.

"Okay, and what do you think would be the result for you if you were to experience not living up to expectations."

Jill smiled. "I would feel bad. Yes, I guess what you're looking for is that tension and uncomfortable sensations would build up in my body. Ah, so since my nervous system knows I would have a hard time tolerating this, the connections to the rational parts of my brain are cut off, making me act more instinctively with a *yes*, not really being able to say *no*, even if this would be the wise thing to do?"

"Exactly, Jill. So, let's imagine that later today your child's teacher sends you an email asking if you can volunteer to oversee an extracurricular activity tomorrow. And let's say you would really like to say no. Knowing what you now know, what might you do when you get the email?"

"I get it! I would stop and do your 3/3 Routine, take a deep breath through my nose, expose and confront the tension and sensations, and maybe realize that whatever the teacher thinks, her thoughts are not really dangerous, and I actually *can* tolerate it. That will keep the connection to the rational parts of my brain open, making me able to say no if I reasoned that this would be the wisest thing to do for myself."

"Brilliant!" said Melanie, showing real excitement as usual.

"Yes, Melanie," said Dr. Krinksted. "And what do you think has actually happened for Jill in this hypothetical situation? What has allowed her to say no?"

"Because she now has true freedom of choice as to whether to do it or not."

"Right again! And let me just underline that I'm not making any judgement regarding if yes or no is the right thing to do for Jill here, only that now Jill truly has a choice as how to respond."

The doctor felt gratified to look at all the faces and see how they were all getting it.

"Even though the real villain is our Performance and Perfection Obsessed Culture, we'll experience it as if it's ourselves creating the problem because we internalize our cultures norms and rules. Then we end up feeling inadequate and stupid for not being superhuman like we've learned we can and should be. Even adding things to our agenda that we really enjoy can add to our stress if we reach the point where we've got way too much to do that feels important and not enough time and energy to do it. And before you know it, we start worrying that maybe we've bitten off more than we can chew—resulting in stress even over things we normally enjoy doing. And it's still the worrying that's the underlying reason for the negative stress.

"It's all part of the same vicious cycle in which the root cause is our inability to tolerate some tension or uncomfortable sensations in our bodies. That is, until we slowly become able to break free by training with the 3 Minute/3 Step Routine."

"Wow," murmured Barbara almost to herself. "It's suddenly very clear to me how worrying about creating a bad vibe really messes up my life in so many ways. I'm definitely up for learning to expose and consciously face up to the discomfort in my body, because if I ever want to become able to make wise decisions—so that I have time and energy for what's most important to me in life—I can see I need to tolerate creating bad vibes." She looked at Alex as she continued, "Not to mention stop blaming Alex for bad thoughts that he's not even having!"

Life isn't about avoiding challenges and problems.

Alex nodded and smiled at his wife.

"Well put, Barbara," said Dr. Krinksted. "Remember folks, life isn't about avoiding challenges and problems; it's about creating a situation where we're able to make the wisest choices regarding which challenges and problems we choose to take upon us, which one to spend our time on—and which ones not to."

"Ah, so is that what you mean by the *without lowering your standards* part of the session title?" asked Laura.

"Yes. Challenges and problems are part of any normal human life. When you are able to recognize and tolerate the discomfort connected with choosing what's most important, including creating the time for this by saying no to what isn't—and even changing your mind if something important changes in you or around you—then you'll be able to use your time and energy wisely. This is really the same as saying you'll learn to break free from the unhealthy societal pressures created by our Performance and Perfection Obsessed Culture. No matter how irrational the beliefs of our unhealthy culture are, they are so ingrained in us that when someone goes against them, it rocks the boat—even when going against them is the wise thing to do."

Dr. Krinksted noticed how a lot of folks in the group looked a little worried. "But here's something even more exciting that will happen. When you learn to expose and tolerate this discomfort that is becoming familiar to you now, you can reach for the stars! Even if you don't achieve the goals you set, you'll be able to tolerate the discomfort that you risk being created in yourself—you know, the feelings of what we usually call failure. Are you with me?"

"I think so," said Rohan. "So, we won't need to lower our dreams just to make sure we avoid the sensations connected to what we usually call failure. Instead, we learn to recognize and confront the sensation—and tolerate it. I'm sure being more able to reach for what's really important to us will also increase our chance of feeling fulfilled, right?"

"Yes, exactly! I love how you're catching on now. It's so simple when you get the hang of it. The root cause of most challenges and problems—in developed countries likes ours where mere survival is generally not an issue anymore—is fear of some discomfort in your body that most people are not even aware of. You're becoming aware of the sensation in a way you never have before, and you now have a method to confront that sensation directly and experience that it's objectively not very dangerous nor completely intolerable. Also, you are learning to tolerate it better. Isn't that exciting?"

Most heads nodded.

"So, what's our homework for this week, Dr. K?" asked Melanie.

"Well between dealing with bad habits and unnecessary stress and worry, I think you have plenty of situations to train with the 3 Minute/3 Step Routine. So, I'm not going to introduce anything new this time. Just carry on consciously exposing and confronting whatever tension and uncomfortable sensations turn up for you around bad habits, stress, and worrying. And I'll look forward to hearing all your experiences next time, which will be in two weeks."

And with that, the screens went dark as everyone said goodbye and logged off one by one.

The Second Virtual Meeting

"Hello everybody," said Dr. Krinksted. "Welcome once again to our virtual meeting. I'm happy with the way we all managed the virtual environment last time, so I'm confident you'll get just as much out of the training as you would if we were still together in person.

"Let's get started—I'm really keen to hear how you've all been doing with consciously recognizing and tolerating the bodily sensations that build up in response to various situations. More importantly, how has it affected your lives?"

Melanie volunteered to start, to nobody's surprise. "Well, since you introduced us to your 3/3 Routine, I can really see how recognizing tensions in my body is becoming a good habit for me. Quite often, I notice that I'm observing what's happening in my body even when it's not directly related to an urge to indulge in a bad habit, nor when I'm worrying or feeling stressed. It's as if I'm just in better contact with myself—if you know what I mean."

"Yes, I know what you mean, Melanie. And how does this affect your life?"

"Pretty much as you said it would. You all know that eating too much chocolate and sweets was the bad habit I used when we were first introduced to the concept of consciously exposing the tension in our bodies by using the 3/3. I still feel I eat more chocolate than is good for me, but I now know exactly the sensations in my body that make me think about chocolate, which in turn makes me reach out for a piece. The sensations are like a restlessness in my body in general, on top of a kind of dryness in my mouth. Even though I sometimes still eat more chocolate than I want to, often I go for quite a few days without really struggling with it."

"Sorry to interrupt you, Melanie, but I want to underline some of what you just said because it was brilliant, and it points to just another thing most people have gotten all wrong. You said that you now know exactly the sensation in your body that makes you think about chocolate, which in turn makes you reach out for a piece. I just had to repeat that because that's really the essence of how our nervous system works; the reason we get the thought of our mood-changing substance or activity—our drug as I call it—into our heads in the first place is that the sensation our nervous system wants to be rid of has shown up in our bodies. And our nervous system knows exactly what it needs us to do to make it go away, so it puts the thought of *our drug* into our heads."

Dr. Krinksted showed his thumbs-up. "When we become aware of what the sensation is and learn to tolerate this sensation, then the thoughts are not put into our heads in the first place. Please continue, Melanie, and sorry for interrupting."

But before Melanie could continue, Laura started talking. "So, what we're getting all wrong is that it's not the thought that comes first and creates the craving; it's the exact opposite. It's the tension that creates the thought about—for instance, chocolate—because Melanie's nervous system knows how chocolate will relieve this tension, right?"

And before the doctor could answer, Laura continued, "So, when we're all so focused on working on our thinking, we're really not working on the root cause. And just like with weeds in a garden, if you're not removing the roots, it's really hard to get rid of the problem." Laura was on a roll and continued. "And your 3/3 Routine solves the problem at the root, because when we are able to expose and tolerate any discomfort that could show up in our bodies, then our nervous system does not have to come up with solutions on how to prevent them or make them go away. Now we can just experience them exactly as they are, uncomfortable or not." Laura took a deep breath, looking around the group, seeming somewhat surprised at herself.

"Spot on, Laura." Dr. Krinksted had a big smile on his face, happy how his new friend might have described his work much better than he could himself.

"Is that why you call it *The Ultimate Life Skill*?"

"We'll have to come back to what *The Ultimate Life Skill* is and how it's related to the 3 Minute/3 Step Routine. We're not quite ready for that yet, Laura, but I promise we'll get there soon."

Dr. Krinksted turned to Melanie, "Sorry that I interrupted you, Melanie. Please continue."

"That's okay. I'm glad I could help. Anyway, what's happening for me is that I feel I'm finding out what role I want sweets to play in my life. And it's really great that I can look at it this way, because even though I hate it when sweets—what you call my drug, my mood-changing activity and substance—have power over me because of that darn tension in me, I also really like sweets and hate to think of giving them up forever."

"So, is it fair to say you feel that you can now use sweets to bring you pleasure in your life without losing control and overindulging in them—what I would call using them instead of overusing or abusing them?"

"Yes, that's it exactly, Dr. K."

"That's great, Melanie. It's so important to become crystal clear when it comes to the difference between use and abuse. There are so many pleasurable things in life, and I think we would be fools if we didn't want to enjoy them. For many people, sweets are one of them. But being able to give us pleasure goes hand in hand with them being able to turn into so-called mood-changing substances or activities. They can all turn into overuse and abuse, and that's when they begin to interfere with our life in negative ways, leading to poor health, poor finances, poor relationships, and other significant issues.

"We want to enjoy chocolate and other foods, but not be unhealthy from overeating. We want to play the odds to make following our favorite sports more exiting, but not empty our bank account gambling. We want to look good and feel good in our clothes, but not shop all the time and end up broke. We want to enjoy a drink or a glass of wine, but we don't want to ruin our health. We want to enjoy intimacy and sex, but not be addicted to it or end up in bed with someone we shouldn't. And I include many other more subtle activities that also activate the pleasurable chemicals in our brains on my list of mood-changing behaviors. I know a lot of my colleagues won't necessarily agree with me on this: We want to help other people, but not ruin our life by being a *pleaser*. We want to warn people off when they cross our boundaries, but we don't want resentment and anger to mess up our life. And the list goes on."

"That makes a lot of sense. I have a friend that exercises so much that I question if it's really good for her. It seems almost like an addiction." Hannah, who wasn't used to sharing a lot, seemed anxious to see how her comment landed.

"Yes, all activities and substances that give us pleasure when we do them or use them can end up taking control of us. We're all victims of this to some extent, and overusing or abusing something creates challenges of different kinds. But the solution is always the same:

consciously exposing and confronting the sensations behind them, so you'll achieve freedom of choice to eat it, drink it, or do it—or not. The more we learn to expose and tolerate discomfort in our bodies, the more we are able to use the long list of things that give us pleasure without ending up overusing or abusing them to an extent that's unhealthy in some way. Okay, let's move on. Who else has something to share?"

"Well, if you don't mind keeping it in the family," said Cliff with a chuckle, "I'll go next. As you all know, my drug, as you call it, is nicotine, and I've had a similar experience to Mel—in fact we've talked about it at home. Even though I don't want to be addicted to smoking, I don't really want to give it up altogether. I'd like to not smoke most days, but I'd still like the freedom to enjoy a few cigarettes when I'm in company, like at parties or barbecues where there are other smokers. But I never thought that was even possible because everyone says if you take just one cigarette after you have quit, it will start up your smoking addiction all over again."

Dr. Krinksted interrupted, "Let me just squeeze in, Cliff, that whoever told you that is not totally off because nicotine is so incredibly addictive that it's practically impossible to reach the goal you just mentioned. But the one way to ever make it possible, if there ever was one, is by learning to tolerate the extreme craving for another cigarette that most former smokers will experience when trying again. So, I would personally not recommend smokers that have quit smoking try to smoke at all because of the high risk they will start smoking daily again."

"Well, for me, just like Mel with her chocolate, I'm beginning to feel this would be possible for me. Already there are days when I don't smoke at all without having to try very hard because I can now tolerate the tension—no more pushing my willpower! It's as if I'm simply able to follow through on what I think is the wise thing for me to do. I don't really think smoking a few cigarettes in any given day or week is really bad for my health—although I know most doctors would disagree. But I think it's the overuse, the addiction part, that's the real killer—in some cases literally."

"Well, one thing is for sure, Cliff. You have gotten to know how the intolerable sensations that used to control you feel. And you've trained yourself to confront them directly, making them more and more tolerable. This will not only help you have a real choice regarding your smoking, but in all aspects of your life. We'll talk more about that later." Dr. Krinksted had a big smile on his face.

Jill stepped into the pause, "I know that storm was not what any of us wanted to go through when we planned our holidays to the island, but I can't tell you how happy I now am that we got stuck there with you, Dr. K—and all of you wonderful people. It has made a world of difference for me that I'm not yelling at my kids as often—and also for them, of course. I just feel so much better about myself.

"I couldn't really admit just how bad it was making me feel, sorry for them and ashamed of myself. But looking back, knowing what I know now, it had a bigger impact on my life than I realized. It's like a whole new world—not being afraid of the next thing they'll do that triggers me or even trying to avoid situations I subconsciously knew would make me feel bad. Especially when we were around other people. It's like a great weight has been taken off my shoulders, literally. I feel as if my shoulders are more relaxed instead of tensed up all the time. What a relief! And it's funny how it has also affected my kids' interactions with each other."

"That's interesting, Jill," said Dr. Krinksted. "How does it affect the way they interact?"

"I think they sometimes wanted my attention, even if that took the form of yelling. I can't explain it, but this is what happened. At first, following your 3/3 Routine, I started just looking at them without yelling, and they looked puzzled because I wasn't doing or saying anything. In the next stage, when they started arguing about who was right and who started the fight, I just paused and listened, maybe talked to them about it, but no yelling. More and more quickly, they would go back to playing together normally. And lately, the teasing has diminished notably. It seems like my yelling was making the situation worse as it became part of a bigger pattern. I'm amazed—and of course extremely happy."

Dr. Krinksted smiled as he answered Jill, "Yes, we're all either part of the problem or part of the solution. In my book, I have a whole chapter on how to use the 3 Minute/3 Step Routine to create and maintain healthy relationships. So, Jill, what happened regarding your stress level?"

"Well, I hadn't really thought about that, but now that you mention it, I can see how my stress level has decreased. I think that's because I don't subconsciously worry that my kids are going to do something that will cause discomfort in my body and end up making me act in a way that makes me feel bad. Now that I know I can tolerate that sensation in my body, I can act more wisely; I don't need to worry about it anymore. The teasing is a natural thing for kids to do now and then, and I can handle it in a way that makes more sense to me—which has definitely reduced my stress level."

"Yes, I think you're right about that, Jill," replied the doctor. "Everything you're going to experience comes from the same root cause, which we all now know is what?"

"A bodily sensation that's hard to tolerate."

"Right. So, you feel better for two reasons: Because you know you can tolerate the discomfort when your kids are acting up and because you don't yell at them as often. They're really two sides of the same coin, and your ability to tolerate that tension in your body is at the root of both things."

"I've also had some interesting experiences around worry, Dr. K," said Diana. "Can I tell you about them?"

"Of course, Diana. The more you all talk about your experiences here, the more you will help yourself and everyone."

"I'm amazed to realize how much I actually do worry about stuff. I've discovered that to some degree, I constantly worry about what people think of me and whether people like me—even people like my mother or my best friends, whom I know love me. In thinking about when I feel that tension we keep talking about—which in my case is usually a subtle feeling of having a lump in my throat—I can now connect a lot of it with saying yes to too much because I don't seem to be able to say no.

"The other day, somebody at work asked if I would be on the committee organizing a client appreciation event. I know from experience the amount of time and work that goes into these things, and I really didn't feel I could squeeze it in. I immediately felt discomfort in my body, but I couldn't say no. I simply couldn't. I knew it was ridiculous, but I found myself agreeing to do it.

"I thought about everything we've been talking about here, observing the sensation in my body as I thought about how this committee work would make my to-do list overflow. Now I understood that the sensation is just that—a bodily sensation—and that it couldn't actually hurt me. So, I went back to my colleague and explained that I really couldn't take on this task, and I asked if she could find someone else. I have to say, the lump in my throat when I approached her felt like a golf ball! But I faced it and followed through.

"Afterwards, I was silently giving myself a huge cheer because it felt so good. This was obviously the wise thing to do for me, but I would never have been able to do it before I learned about your 3/3 Routine and experienced it with my bad habit."

Dr. Krinksted smiled and looked very happy. "I love seeing people experience for themselves the huge effects that can come from consciously facing this discomfort in our bodies. Diana, this isn't really important, but I'm curious to know how your colleague reacted."

"Just as most people probably would. She said of course it wasn't a problem, and she would find someone else for the task. And I really felt she was sincere in not wanting me to stress out over this. It's ridiculous how often I worry for no good reason, and I'm sure this goes for a lot of people."

"It's not really ridiculous, Diana," the doctor said. "As I've said before, it's just a function of our nervous systems watching out for real danger and helping us avoid it. So, like I've said, worrying is really our friend. It's only when we do it too much that it becomes unhealthy, just like overdoing things that bring us pleasure.

"If our nervous system must overwork in its attempt to predict what situations might cause intolerable sensations in the future and how to avoid those scenarios, we end up worrying a lot. Can you see how this normal function of our nervous system is such a bad cocktail when mixed with the invisible villain of our Performance and Perfection Obsessed Culture? That mix makes us interpret not living up to all the unrealistic expectations that we put on each other and ourselves as real danger?"

Dr. Krinksted didn't wait for an answer. "But if we become able to tolerate these sensations, then we will automatically be more relaxed and at ease. Do you understand what I'm saying?"

"I'm not sure I do," said Phil. "Can you give us some more examples?"

"Sure, let me give you a few hypothetical examples. Let's say that you and Elinor are arranging a picnic. You think that if the weather is bad, it will ruin the whole thing. In 3/3 words, your nervous system knows that the tension you will experience in your body if the weather is bad will be hard to tolerate. Every day your mind reminds you to check the weather forecast and makes you wonder what you'll do if the weather is bad. In short, you'll worry, right?"

"Right."

"On the other hand, Elinor's nervous system knows that if the weather is bad on the day of the picnic, she'll have a certain amount of tension, but it won't be hard for her to tolerate. So, her nervous system doesn't have to work hard to help her avoid it. It doesn't put the thought into her head to check the weather forecast and doesn't make her wonder what she'll do if the weather turns bad. So, she doesn't worry. She'll be more relaxed.

"In situations like this, we might say it's because one partner cares more about the weather than the other, but in fact, the root cause is something else: the nervous system trying to avoid an intolerable bodily sensation.

"Here's an example at the other end of the spectrum. Let's say we have a couple who are privileged people: good jobs, good financial situation, good lifestyle. The husband could never see himself not having this lifestyle, not having the prestige they enjoy. Seen from the point of view of discomfort and tension in the body, his nervous system knows that if he were to lose any of this, the tension would be unbearable. The result is that he worries a lot about whether his boss might fire him, whether his stock market investments will crash, etc.

"On the other hand, his wife knows that she could easily live under different circumstances. Her sister makes much less money than she does, lives in a modest home in a suburb, and is perfectly happy. The wife feels she'd be quite happy in those circumstances too. Result: Her nervous system doesn't put the thought into her head that a lifestyle change could make her unhappy, so she doesn't worry.

"Remember, the nervous system is always looking out for situations that would create bodily sensations that are hard to tolerate. If you can get to a point where it knows you can tolerate most any sensation in any circumstance, you simply won't worry or not as much. In the case of this couple, she has reached that point, and he hasn't, with predictable results."

"And here's the thing, if all the husband did was becoming better at tolerating the discomfort, he would also not worry so much."

"Thanks for the examples," said Phil. "I get what you're saying in principle, and I think I need to experience it more for myself to really believe it. Sorry!"

"You're right about that, Phil. We all have to experience this for ourselves again and again to accept that it's true. Just keep confronting the sensation of tension when you worry, and you'll slowly be able to tolerate it more. And your nervous system's need to arrange your circumstances in a specific way to avoid tension will, slowly but surely, start to diminish."

CHAPTER 5

How to Stop Self-Criticism:

Forgiveness, Part 1

"I think you're all ready to up the ante even more now, so I'm going to introduce the next topic: how to use the 3 Minute/3 Step Routine to stop self-criticism and guilt-tripping ourselves."

Melanie sat forward in her chair and exclaimed, "Yes! I looked in the table of contents, and I've been waiting for this part. People usually don't think this about me, but I'm always criticizing or blaming myself for something."

"Me too," said Barbara. Others nodded their heads as well.

"Good," said Dr. Krinksted. "Then you're going to find this life-changing because you'll finally understand deep in your bones that there's nothing wrong with you and that you're always doing the best you can—even when it might not seem that way and you're not living up to your own or other people's expectations.

"So, as usual, I'll give you a short introduction to the subject, and we'll go deeper into it next time we meet, when you have had some experience of it in your own life through training with the 3 Minute/3 Step Routine.

"As we've discussed before, worrying is really our friend because it protects us from bad things that could happen to us. It's both normal and good that our nervous systems analyze possible scenarios for what danger they might present. If we didn't do this, if this ability wasn't deeply rooted in our nervous systems, we could miss real dangers and die. But as we also discussed, it's the *unnecessary* worrying we want to reduce, the worrying that's based on beliefs that aren't true or aren't true anymore, because that's what affects our lives negatively."

"Like the false beliefs that are ingrained in us by our Performance and Perfection Obsessed Culture?" Melanie interjected.

"Yes, that's right, Melanie. A lot of these twisted or false beliefs come from our unhealthy culture. What you're about to experience is that self-criticism and being hard on yourself are just extensions of this worrying. It's simply your nervous system trying to prevent you from doing something or repeat doing something that would produce that almost unbearable tension in your body that it misinterprets as dangerous. To a certain extent, this is healthy. But when your nervous system is working hard to prevent you from doing anything that creates tension and sensations in your body despite those things not being really dangerous, this pattern becomes unhealthy and what we experience as too much self-criticism or being too hard on ourselves.

"Okay, so here's how I want you to include this in your practice. The doctor shared his screen showing a slightly new version of the 3/3 Routine.

The 3 Minute/3 Step Routine for
Reducing Self-criticism

Step 1: Stop and observe

As you all know by now, the first step of the 3/3 Routine is to stop and observe. So, any time you experience negative self-criticism and guilt-tripping yourself, I want you to stop, take a deep breath through your nose, and observe the tension or uncomfortable sensations in your body, and observe what the voices in your head are saying to you.

As usual, what you'll be observing when you stop are the tension and sensations in your body and the thoughts that run through your mind.

Step 2: Pause and observe

While you pause for as long as you like, keep observing the thoughts that run through your mind and how the tension or uncomfortable sensations you observed in your body in step 1 might be building up in strength, or if new tension or uncomfortable sensations are emerging in your body. And again, while you pause, don't hesitate to take some deep breaths as this will help you in your endeavor.

Remember that the 3/3 Routine is not a training of your willpower; it's a training of your ability to observe. Make the pause as long as you like while observing what is happening in your body and mind without trying to change anything while you're observing.

Step 3: Continue and observe

When you don't feel like pausing any longer, observe how the tension and sensations in your body and the thoughts running through your mind change as you continue your activity where you left off before starting this specific 3/3 Routine.

"I see we've run a few minutes over our time today, so let's stop here. If you have any questions, you can always email me. Otherwise, I look forward to seeing you all again two weeks from now."

Before leaving his office, Dr. Krinksted added a few extra notes about the participants on his sheet of paper.

Notes:

Melanie, Melanie's mother, Irene, and Melanie's father, Cliff

Melanie

Thirty-one years old.

The enthusiastic young woman who reached out to me and initiated our group meeting. Bought the book because she wants to break a bad habit.

But also want to better understand how our Performance and Perfection Obsessed Culture messes up her life, and how she can break away from it more. Likes that it's all based on neuroscience.

Bad habit: Has a sweet tooth.

Has started recognizing different sensations related to her cravings for sweets.

Described the sensations she experiences like a restlessness in her body and dryness in her mouth. Even though she still eats more chocolate than she wants to, often she doesn't really struggle with it anymore. She feels like she can now use sweets to bring her pleasure in her life without losing control and overindulging in them (without resulting in overuse or abuse).

Has started noticing that she's observing what's happening in her body even when it's not directly related to an urge to indulge in her bad habit nor when she's worrying or feeling stressed. She calls this being in better contact with herself.

Mentioned that she's also experiencing a lot of self-criticism.

Irene, Melanie's mother

Showed up to support her daughter. She is a physician, and she wants to make sure what her daughter is into is something sound and rational. As a physician, she's also open to learning something new that might allow her to better help the stressed patients in her clinic.

Nothing new.

Nothing new.

Cliff, Melanie's father

Told us that his daughter, Melanie, talked him into joining.

Bad habit: Smoking.

Has tried to quit many times but never succeeded. This is what he's using the 3/3 Routine to work on.

Has already experienced that beating his bad habit using the 3/3 Routine instead of trying to use his willpower works in a totally different manner. Has really started to gain a whole new experience of all the tension and thoughts related to his bad habit of smoking (his craving for nicotine) via the 3/3 Routine. It has become obvious to him that the real reason he smokes is not the pleasure it gives him, but the tension and uncomfortable sensations he never noticed before when he reaches out for a cigarette—and how his urge for a cigarette increases in strength when this tension and sensations increase.

He's also catching on to how our Performance and Perfection Obsessed Culture is a real villain in our lives but still something that each of us can break free from when we learn how.

Told us that he can't wait to see how this will help him in more areas of his life when we get to that.

Told us that if there was just one thing he could change in his life it would be to experience less stress and worry.

Alex and Barbara

They are probably in their forties.

Alex

The guy I heard complaining at the reception desk. He said he showed up because he didn't have anything better to do. He generally seems to have a bad temper, and he's very skeptical. He was the one who almost left when I mentioned the notion that free will is an illusion. I think he might be more stressed than he is aware of, and I got the impression that he's not very open to trying to see things in a new way no matter how true or wise they are.

Nothing new.

Alex seems to have changed, and his skepticism has vanished because what he is learning is helping him regarding the stress he is now telling us about. Also realizes how his stress is affecting his wife and their relationship.

Barbara

Didn't say much. Seemed embarrassed by Alex's temper and behavior.

Nothing new.

Has realized she worries practically all the time—from the smallest things to the worst things she can imagine (she mentioned divorce). Sometimes feels she's going crazy. Her worrying is connected to Alex's temper and behavior, and the risk of creating a bad vibe messes up her life in many ways, not only with Alex. She understands that she needs to learn to tolerate creating bad vibes so she can make wise decisions. Then, she will have time and energy for what's most important in her life.

Barbara seemed happy that it appears what they are learning is changing her husband. And their speaking openly about this created a good connection between them. I noticed that Alex reached out and took Barbara's hand when she spoke about all this.

Also mentioned that she's always criticizing or blaming herself for something.

Rohan and Harini

They are here with their young daughter.

Rohan

The guy I saw sitting in the lobby flirting with a woman when his wife and daughter entered. He did the introduction of his wife.

Bad habit: Checking his inbox all the time.

Told us of another bad habit—constant phone checking—uses the 3/3 Routine for this.

Rohan seems to be more and more interested and is participating in what he's learning here.

Harini

Didn't say much.

Bad habit: Nail biting. Told us that she hates herself for—and is embarrassed by—her lack of self-control.

Has started noticing something new when doing the 3/3 Routine, but hasn't yet exposed exactly what the tension and uncomfortable sensations related to her nail biting are.

Seems interested in learning more.

Nothing new.

Diana

The red-haired woman who was the object of Rohan's attentions in the lobby. She is travelling by herself.

Mentioned her inability to relax. The 3/3 Routine has made her aware of the tension and sensations that are connected to this. She uses alcohol to relax and has started using the 3/3 Routine to gain more control of this.

Has discovered that, to some degree, she constantly worries about what people think of her and whether people like her. Even the ones closest to her. Can now connect a lot of saying yes to too much and inability to say no to the tension I point to, which in her case is usually a subtle feeling of having a lump in her throat. Feels it's ridiculous how often she worries for no good reason.

Elinor and Phil

The stylish, blond woman and the man that I saw in the dining area that had the discussion about her shopping and his eating habits.

They have a six-year-old girl and a twelve-year-old boy.

At the meeting, I felt tension between them.

Elinor

Introduced both of them.

Seems like she already really likes my teachings and the 3/3 Routine.

Nothing new.

Phil

Said that Elinor dragged him along to our meeting.

Seems to have also caught interest in what I'm teaching. He mentioned that he's using the 3/3 when the urge for reaching for a bag of potato chips or a second burger shows up.

Has really caught interest now. Told us it has been an eye-opener how often he has tension in his body that he wasn't aware of before affecting his level of self-control.

Named his bad habit: Eat too much and too often.

Told us that his food cravings give him a short fuse. Can be a bit of a bear at work, and easily loses his temper.

Laura and Hannah

The young couple.

Laura

The inquisitive one who is doing a master's in psychology.

Has a strong professional interest in everything I teach.

Reaching for a deep understanding of how our nervous system works and the implications of this.

Hannah

Didn't say much. Was introduced by her fiancée, Laura.

Still hasn't shared or asked anything.

Has started sharing her thoughts.

Jill

The woman who asked the question about being triggered when her two young daughters tease each other. She's alone with them here on vacation.

It was Jill I had the private talk with. Uses the 3/3 Routine when being triggered when her two young daughters tease each other.

When starting the topic on unnecessary stress and worry, she said that her name was written all over that topic.

Told us a few things this time: She feels ashamed when yelling at her daughters, but also that this yelling has decreased, which makes her feel much better about herself. Feels it's also good for her daughters

that she doesn't yell as often and it even makes them tease each other less, which has decreased her stress level.

Under the topic of stress and worry, told us that she's saying yes to more than she has time and energy for because she wants to live up to societal expectations and wants people to like her and not think badly of her.

Finally, she also mentioned she started to feel more grounded since starting this training.

Yan

The oldest guy who sat in the back. Didn't share anything yet.

Still hasn't shared or asked anything yet.

Nothing new.

The Third Virtual Meeting

One by one, all the participants popped up on the screens until everyone was there, and Dr. Krinksted greeted them all. "Hello everyone, and welcome back for our third virtual meeting. It's been about six weeks now since we first got together as a group on the island, and I'm wondering how you're all doing?"

"I'm doing great," said Phil. "Before we went on vacation, I felt so bored with all the daily routines of my work and my life, but now I'm glad to have them back."

"I couldn't agree more," said Diana. "But I think what you're asking is how it's going with our training of consciously noticing and confronting distress in our bodies when it happens, right?"

"Well both really—and I hope there's some correlation between the two."

Barbara, who was gradually becoming more comfortable speaking up in the group, responded, "For me, as I get back to my normal life, this routine of consciously exposing and confronting the tension in my body has become more of a challenge. It's really easy to fall into the trap of doing what I always do without awareness of what's happening in my body and in my mind. Sometimes I feel like I'm living my life on autopilot."

"Yes," agreed Diana. "It's kind of frightening how one day just follows the last, and time just seems to fly by quickly."

Dr. Krinksted nodded at everyone and smiled. "Yes, that's what our lives typically looks like when we haven't yet built the conscious habit of awareness into our lives. I'll speak more about this and how this affects our lives negatively when we get to the final chapters of the book."

"I am actually experiencing the opposite of you guys," said Rohan, smiling. "And I think it's because of training with your 3/3 Routine, Dr. K. It's like it's made me become used to constantly having some part of my awareness on what happens *in* me, in my body and mind, and I can honestly say it has changed my life already."

Dr. Krinksted couldn't hide how happy he was while answering, "That's very encouraging, Rohan. Could you tell us a little more about what you mean?"

"The bad habit I chose to work on after our first meeting was gambling. It wasn't hard at first because, as we all know, we had no access to the internet. For some of you, not having internet was a problem because it affected your typical daily routines, but for me, it just meant I couldn't indulge in my bad habit.

"As soon as I could go online again, I've been consciously facing that familiar sensation of discomfort connected to the urge to gamble. Using your 3/3 Routine has slowly given me a new level of control. Occasionally, I still gamble more than I might like to, but now it's more like a small bad habit. Something I use for enjoyment. Not to get rid of tension, because I can tolerate the tension now, so I don't have to get rid of it at all costs . . . so to speak," Rohan smiled.

"That's great news, Rohan."

"Yes, it is, Doc, but there's something else that's much more important to me. I haven't talked about this before. But there is an area of my life I'm definitely ashamed of, that I did criticize myself for, and that I've never been able to get control of—until now. After getting in touch with what is happening in my body in general, I realized the same mechanism was playing out in a much more serious area of my life."

Rohan stopped for a moment, looking at his wife and seeming to gather strength from her encouraging smile. "Harini and I talked about this, and she's fully in support of me bringing this out into the open in the context of what we're learning."

The group became quieter and even more attentive than usual, sensing that Rohan was about to say something private and important to him.

"Some of you experienced this personally while we were at the resort—I flirt a lot. Some people might think this is not a big deal, but unfortunately, during the eleven years we've been married, it hasn't always stopped at harmless flirtation. I've actually been unfaithful a few times."

Even though he experienced severe discomfort, Rohan persevered with his story. "I always felt I wasn't able to resist it. I simply couldn't help myself, so it wasn't my fault—at least that's what I told myself. I've been able to resist the actual physical part, the affairs, for several years now—the fear of losing Harini and our family forced me to resist. But the energy is still there, and the flirting is still happening, and I'm always afraid I'll fall into the trap again. You can probably guess what I'm going to tell you now."

Dr. Krinksted smiled empathetically, having heard similar stories so many times before.

"As I've developed the habit of consciously experiencing the sensations in my body, it's become obvious to me what drives this behavior. The happy result is that whenever I feel tempted to indulge in flirtatious behavior, whether in person or on social media, I silently go through your 3/3 Routine. Slowly but surely, I'm getting better at tolerating the discomfort and getting back in control of the behavior— acting wisely as you call it."

Rohan looked around his screen a little sheepishly, clearly wondering if he had been right to share this particular information. But their smiles and nods reassured him.

Phil held up his hand for a virtual high-five. "Good for you, man," he said.

"That's really great, Rohan," said Melanie, a serious look on her young face. She had in fact been one of the objects of Rohan's flirtatious behavior on the island, but she didn't dare mention that for fear that her father wouldn't react well.

"Yes, well done, Rohan," said Dr. Krinksted. "I'm happy you told us this, and I can admit that I've been there myself. In fact, it's a great place for me to give you another aspect of how we're controlled and how we can change habits and behavior.

"As we've discussed before, the notion of free will isn't true. How our brains work is extremely complex, but for the purpose of understanding and using this knowledge, the simplified version is that we are always controlled by the interaction of two major forces within us: the pull from the rational parts of our brains and the pull from the more primitive parts of our brains. The first one is closely related to what we experience as our will and willpower, and the latter is more closely related to our instinctive behavior and to getting our more basic needs and immediate pleasures satisfied. To gain true freedom of choice on how to behave, you must work on both these forces.

"The problem is that in our Performance and Perfection Obsessed Culture, we really have only focused on the willpower part. And this leaves us with a high percentage of actions that we can't control or resist because, as you know by now, if the more primitive parts of our brains deem it necessary, it can shut off the connections to the rational parts of our brains, taking our willpower out of the equation no matter how strongly we've developed it. I don't care how well-meaning, sensible, or well-educated you are, if you haven't made it a routine to consciously expose and confront discomfort in your body, you'll have a too high percentage of actions in which you're in much less control than you could be."

"Let me just make sure I'm getting this right, Dr. K," said Laura. "You're saying that if there's a lot of tension in my body that I have a hard time tolerating—whether I'm aware of it or not— this will pull me in the direction of acting more primitively and instinctively. So, I would need a huge amount of willpower from the start to stay in control—to act wisely as you call it?"

Dr. Krinksted nodded.

The illusion is that we are in control of our nervous systems, but it's our nervous systems that are in control of us.

"And when I have exposed and confronted this tension directly so that I can tolerate it better—no matter if the tension is still there or not—then I need much less willpower—sometimes none at all—to stay in control?"

"Yes, I think that's a fair way to describe it."

"And the way my nervous system creates this situation is by impairing my brain's ability to use my willpower. So that no matter how much willpower I'm able to muster, the force of my nervous system to fight intolerable tension will always win, because that force can simply cut the connection to my willpower altogether if it wants to? Would that be a good way of interpreting what you're saying?"

"Yes," said Dr. Krinksted, nodding. "Of course, this is oversimplifying things for the matter of making it usable, but for all practical purposes, that's how we're wired. We're really back where we started—the illusion of free will. The illusion is that we are in control of our nervous systems, but it's actually the other way around; it's our nervous systems that are in control of us. But the more you do the 3 Minute/3 Step Routine and let your nervous system experience what are signs of real danger—and what are not—it will become better at allowing the connection to the rational parts of your brain to stay open. Bottom line, your willpower will be more in front of running the show."

Jill raised her hand. "So, the primitive parts of my brain are like the board of a company, and my willpower is the CEO?" Jill asked and continued, "The CEO is only in power as long as the board is happy with what's going on . . . as soon as the board wants something else, they can take all the power away from the CEO instantly and overrule, no matter if this CEO is objectively doing a good job or not."

"Yes, that's a great analogy for people who know how big companies work. And like I have said before, our species would never have come this far if we weren't designed like this, for better and for worse. And it's not really our nervous systems that are the villains here; it's our unhealthy culture in which so many of the things that are actually normal for us are looked upon as weaknesses or being wrong, making us react in fear. I hope your training here has already helped make you aware of that and enabled you to start breaking free from this."

"Right," rejoined Alex. "So, all we have to do is simply start exposing and confronting the discomfort in our bodies by using your 3/3 Routine in the way we're already doing with regard to our bad habits and unnecessary worry?"

"Precisely," said Dr. Krinksted with a broad smile. "And let me just insert here that the 3 Minute/3 Step Routine is just one way to attain this. Anything that makes you more aware of and able to tolerate the tension in your body will give you the same results. And I'm glad you used the word *simply* because the 3/3 Routine really is that, and it's the simplest way I have found to get the results. I know how it might be hard to understand the magnitude of the benefits of this because it goes against the beliefs that have been ingrained in us growing up: that if we don't struggle, there's something wrong. But yes, it really is simple."

"But not necessarily easy," said Melanie, "because it's so deeply ingrained in us, right?"

"Correct, Melanie. Correct, Alex. I'm so happy that I really can convey this information and training in a workshop setting like this!" said Dr. Krinksted enthusiastically. "Every time we meet, I experience how you are grasping it at a deeper level.

"There's a constant fight in all of us between our willpower and the force always working to prevent discomfort in our bodies. That's just how we're wired, and there's nothing we can do to change it. But we can change how much and how often our willpower is impaired, so that we only react instinctively when there's a good reason for this. When confronted with real and immediate danger."

Diana raised her hand and took a second or two before speaking, "I'm beginning to understand how pervasive this must be in my life. I'm looking forward to hearing about how this affects all the other aspects and areas of my life that we'll be exploring."

"Yes, Diana. In fact, this is the cause of pretty much all the unnecessary suffering we experience in our part of the world, where mere survival is generally not an issue anymore. It's heartbreaking that most of the suffering in our rich and privileged lives is caused by something we do to ourselves, so to speak. Until we really *get* this, we'll keep seeing ourselves as inadequate with voices in our heads full of self-criticism and guilt. You know how tough it is believing you should be superhuman when you are just human. It becomes a continuous struggle to live up to unrealistic expectations.

"The good news is that all this will change as you slowly increase your ability to be consciously present to both the hard-to-tolerate stuff and the pleasurable stuff. It will take you off autopilot. You'll eventually end up experiencing a full and rich life, which is what most people really yearn for. This is what I call the ultimate life benefit of this training, and we'll come back to this later. I'll tell you that if all you ever did was incorporate the simple routine of exposing and confronting the tension and sensations in your bodies when they happen, that would still have a more positive effect on your lives than you can imagine."

After the pause that followed this, Rohan began to speak thoughtfully, "I must admit it was scary for me to talk so openly with you all about my flirting, but I'm glad I did because this makes so much sense to me now. I really understand how this mechanism is the root cause of all the behaviors I struggle with, not just the flirting."

"Yes, I appreciate you taking the risk of making yourself vulnerable, Rohan, because all the sharing helps make it easier for everybody to understand. The fear you experienced before you shared your story was once again that fear of distress that would follow in your body, distress that your nervous system doesn't want you to face. But when you felt certain you would be able to tolerate it, you were able to speak up. I'll talk about the importance of being able to make ourselves vulnerable later when we get to the topic of healthy relationships. Please remind me if I forget, Rohan. Does anyone want to comment on this?"

Diana leaned forward in her seat. "Well, I'm one of those who felt your need to attract the attention of women. Thanks for sharing your story, Rohan, as it helps me understand this whole question of how we are all pushed to do irrational things that don't serve anyone—*unwise* as we call it here. When you shared your story, Rohan, you said that you felt you weren't able to resist being unfaithful, that you couldn't help yourself, so it wasn't your fault. When you said that, I must admit it made me a little angry. But now, I understand how that's really true, and not only for you in this case, but for all of us. We all end up behaving in irrational ways we really don't want to, but can't help but do, because deep down we are controlled by our nervous system and not our willpower. What we're sharing here is really profound. I feel there's a lot at stake for me in many areas of my life."

"Can I change the subject, Dr. K?" asked Phil. Without waiting for an answer, he continued, "Elinor and I have used our own version of the 3/3 Routine with our kids. We're trying to get them to become better at tolerating cravings—the tension in their bodies—by postponing what they crave—candy for our six-year-old and games on the iPad for our twelve-year old."

"Sure, please continue, Phil."

"Well, all we're doing is making them wait just a little before giving in."

"Sounds interesting. Any observations?"

"Not yet. But it seems they don't mind so much as long as we don't make them wait too long."

"That's funny," said Melanie. "I've been doing something similar with my friend's four-year-old daughter. I've made up a little game of how long she can tolerate being tickled. I tickle her lightly at the beginning and then increase the intensity. It's just great fun, but I realize now how I'm training her to tolerate the tension the tickling creates in her body. Of course, I'm not holding her in any way while we play this game, so she can stop the game freely at any moment she wants. Do you think it's a good idea, Dr. K?"

"Yes, I do, Melanie. Any way we can become better at tolerating tension and uncomfortable sensations in our bodies will help in this direction, like the 3 Minute/3 Step Routine. There's another reason this makes our lives better—I'll be discussing that before we end our session today. But before that, I'd like to hear from more of you who have had experiences around self-criticism and blame. Anybody?"

"I've had an extremely valuable insight with this round of training your 3/3 Routine," said Jill. "Most of my adult life—both at work and in social situations—if someone disagrees with something I've said, I take it as criticism. From a rational standpoint, I know it's just someone else's viewpoint, but my body reacts like I said something stupid. I often hold back from saying what's on my mind, and I know that has not done my career any good. Sometimes I don't voice an idea at a meeting, and then someone else says it and everyone agrees. Then I criticize myself for not speaking up.

"Since I started working with your 3/3 Routine on this, I've had the strangest experience. When I criticize myself, I seem to hear this little voice at a specific place inside my head, at the back right here," she said, pointing to the back of her head. "It says the same things over and over: *You're so stupid; why don't you shut up and not let everyone know how stupid you are?* It's obvious now that this voice has been there all along; I just haven't been aware of it. Now that I am aware, I hear it all the time, and I'm still surprised each time. It's strange how it's so specific and has had such an impact on me—and I never noticed it before. No wonder I hold back from sharing my ideas!"

"Yes," said Dr. Krinksted. "Like we've talked about before, we all have voices in our heads, our inner dialogue. But very often it's really a monologue. And it's amazing how little voices can worm their way in and affect how we're feeling and make us feel even worse than we did already, telling us something that increases or creates more tension and uncomfortable sensations. As you're becoming more aware of these voices, you will notice how this inner dialogue is always an integral part of the tension and sensations that are happening in your bodies. Experiencing how you speak to yourself is extremely valuable for this reason."

"But what are these voices in our heads, Dr. K, and how do they start?"

"They're really just thoughts, Jill. We can see our thoughts as a discussion between all kinds of positions and perspectives, analyzing and discussing all the information we pick up from within ourselves and from our environment and connecting all this with our past experiences and learnings. Thoughts, voices in your head, inner dialogue—they are different words for the same thing. And of course, I'm sure you know by now the whole purpose of all this analyzing, yes?"

Predictably, it was Melanie who jumped in with the answer, "How to avoid situations that create the sensations of discomfort in our bodies."

"Right, Melanie."

"That's my girl!" said Cliff.

"And the reason the nervous system reacts this way is that it interprets intolerable tension and sensations in our bodies as dangerous, as a possible threat to our thriving or survival. That's why it's such a strong force that it can and will make the primitive parts of our brains hijack us when we interpret something as a threat, even when it's not. Remember Barbara's fear of spiders? Of course, an ordinary little spider isn't going to harm her, but her nervous system acts as if it could and takes over control."

As he often did, Dr. Krinksted stopped talking and gave them a moment to absorb what he'd said. "One more point on this," the doctor continued. "As human beings, we start life as merely responsive beings, dependent on almost only the primitive parts of the brain before the more rational parts develop. The function of the rational parts of the brain is to help the primitive parts behave in a way that increases chances of thriving and surviving. But even though it's really a cooperation, it often ends up more like a fight: For example, *I shouldn't reveal what my friend just told me . . .* but deep inside, something in me wants me to do it to relieve tension. *Too much candy is not good for me . . .* but deep inside, something in me wants my hand to reach out for the chocolate cake to give me a pleasurable feeling. I'm sure you all have your own version of such a fight.

"What you just told us, Jill, is another example. If you didn't have the little voice of your thoughts to affect you, the more primitive part of you would just start speaking your thoughts without worry. But because you've experienced bad feelings from speaking up, this has laid the ground for the nervous system to help you avoid intolerable tension in your body. So, it takes the form of the little voice telling you to shut up. And of course it works, because you end up not speaking up, and this prevents other people's responses from making you feel bad again."

"So, how can you say that this is not a sign that our nervous system doesn't fit in our modern way of living?" asked the inquisitive Laura.

"Well, our thoughts are really our friends. But right now, we're focusing on when they get in our way—when they are misinterpreting the danger level at any given moment—making us act irrational in the situation instead of wise. It might be hard to believe, but most of the time our thinking, our voices are helping us. In people that are unfortunate enough to have brain damage, like a stroke, those voices may disappear for a while, and these folks experience the absence of this help.

"One man who lost his inner voice thought it was fantastic at first because all the self-criticism stopped, but he ended up really missing the help of this voice after a while. One of the examples he gave was when shopping for groceries and forgetting his shopping list. When this used to happen, he realized it was a little voice in his head that reminded him what was on the list, and now that this voice was gone, he couldn't remember. You'll experience how these voices in your head are really trying to help you as best they can when you increase your awareness of what they are telling you. The same goes for the tension and uncomfortable sensations—the bodily part of what we could call our anxiety or distress—as they are also our friends. And, just as in the case of friends in our external lives, we have to listen to and closely examine what they're saying and see if it rings true for us. Am I making any sense here?"

Most people nodded.

"I've often been asked what comes first—the thoughts or the sensation of discomfort. Even though I've said before that it's the tension and sensations that are at the root, it all happens almost at the same time and quickly moves forward. That's why you have to observe it all so closely, over and over again, to discern what's really happening.

"Of course, it all falls apart when your nervous system misinterprets what's happening. After all, not being liked or even being labeled stupid is not actually life-threatening, at least in most parts of the world. Yet, our nervous systems still act as if we are in danger—unless and until we make it experience that the tension isn't a sign of real danger by consciously exposing and confronting it. Just for the record, a lot of consciously exposing and confronting happens automatically, all the time. Just think of all the things we've been nervous about or afraid of as kids. It's an integral part of growing up and happens all by itself, just by living life. All I'm telling you to do is force it to happen where it hasn't happened yet. That's a big part of what the 3 Minute/3 Step Routine is all about, forcing this to happen.

"Okay, back to what we were talking about. I got carried away again. So it takes a lot of repeated experience for our nervous system to de- and relearn, which is what the 3/3 Routine is forcing it to do. And on top of this, we make our nervous system learn from experience that tension and sensations that used to be intolerable can now be tolerated, so it doesn't have to try so hard to make us avoid these sensations. When our nervous system stops trying so hard to avoid these sensations from happening this is what we experience as less self-criticism and less guilt-tripping ourselves. We also start acting more wisely because the connections to the rational parts of our brains stay open—and acting more wisely also diminishes this criticism and blame. All in all, that's basically why training with the 3 Minute/3 Step Routine starts the positive upward spiral in the context of stopping self-criticism and blame.

"Are you still with me?" Dr. Krinksted looked at all the faces on his screen.

Laura's face expanded on his screen when she started talking. "In the headline for this chapter you have the word *forgiveness*. How does that fit into this equation?"

"Thanks for reminding me about the forgiveness part, Laura," Dr. Krinksted smiled while gesturing "the citations" with his hands.

"When doing the 3/3 Routine again and again, day after day, in more and more aspects and areas of your life, an awareness sinks into your bones that you have anything but free will—you're always under the influence of the primitive parts of your brain that's able to hijack you for no good reason. You'll gain a deep understanding that you're doing the best you can and that there's nothing wrong with you even when you're not proud of your behavior or you don't live up to your own values or rules—not to mention the rules of our unhealthy culture! As this happens, you'll start forgiving yourself without even having to try."

Melanie cut in, "So when Rohan told himself that it wasn't his fault, he was right? He really was a victim of his nervous system, and we all are. All we can do is try to gain as much control as possible by exposing and confronting sensations in our bodies, so our rational minds are being disconnected as little as possible?"

"Yes, what Rohan felt was right. He was at the mercy of the primitive parts of his brain at the time. But not anymore, because he has learned to tolerate the tension that drove this behavior."

Laura started speaking again, "So, when you say we tolerate it better, that happens because when we keep confronting the tension that is exposed in the 3/3 Routine, we start taking the discomfort for what it really is: something that may feel awful and almost unbearable but won't actually harm us. So, our nervous system doesn't feel it has to be removed quickly, no matter the consequences?"

"Right, Laura! That's a good way of putting it. Do you all follow this?"

Most of the group nodded, some vigorously and others more slowly and thoughtfully.

"It's simple, but that doesn't mean it's easy. It can be difficult to explore and understand. It takes time and effort to expose and confront all the different kinds of sensations that are being misinterpreted that prevents us from reacting wisely in different parts of our lives. You need to set aside a little time each day to do the 3 Minute/3 Step training for its long-term results. Most people are just interested in quick fixes, but I'm sure you all know they never really work in the long term. You need to persevere to reap the benefits. But it's so worthwhile—as you've all started to experience by now.

"Okay, this has been fascinating, and I'm very happy with your observations and how you have shared them with one another. I apologize for not being able to convey this better this time, but now it's time for me to give you a short introduction to the next area you're going to include in your training.

"I've called the next chapter *Aim for Effortless, Not for Easy*. Can't wait to share with you how the 3/3 Routine will enable you to find common ground between what you feel like doing and what you think you should do, without the usual inner conflict that most of us know so well."

CHAPTER 6

Aim for Effortless, Not for Easy

"Okay," said Dr. Krinksted. "*Aim for Effortless, Not for Easy* is the next area of your life in which you're going to start exposing that now familiar sensation of tension in your body. So, let me try to explain what I mean by that.

"When desiring to break free from a Performance and Perfection Obsessed Culture, it would be natural to think that the opposite of being obsessed with working hard and making things perfect would be to forget about performing at your best and striving for perfection altogether. In other words, lower all your goals so your life will be easy. But nothing could be further from the truth. The thing is: it's not the performance and perfection that's the problem; it is the *obsession*. Wanting to do well and create stuff is a normal and integral part of human nature. We love to experience using the abilities we have, learning new skills, and enjoying and celebrating what we create and who we've become in the process. So, if we just lower our goals, this won't necessarily make us feel better about ourselves and our lives."

Knowing that he often talked more than people could take in when speaking about subjects that were near to his heart, the doctor looked around the group and didn't continue until he sensed that people were ready for more. "So, how do we break free from our Performance and Perfection Obsessed Culture in a way that doesn't take this important part of our life experience away from us?

Melanie responded with a big smile on her face, "Well, I think I have the answer because you gave it away when we started. By aiming for effortless and not for easy. But I have no idea what you mean by that."

"Right, so let me explain. I'll start with *effortless*. The way I use this term in this context, I'm only considering the mental part. *Effortless* means doing something without inner resistance, without an inner conflict. So, what you're doing might be extremely strenuous, but as long as there's no inner conflict regarding whether you should be doing this or be doing something else, I'll still call it *effortless* in this context. Doing something that requires almost no energy at all but creates all kinds of inner conflicts regarding whether you should be doing it—or if you should spend your time on something else instead—can feel like a huge effort.

"On the other hand, the way I use the term *easy* in the context of aiming for effortless, not for easy, I'm referring to the total exertion something requires." Dr. Krinksted looked closely to check if the group seemed to follow his thoughts.

Laura raised her hand. "So, you're telling us to go for what we can do wholeheartedly—no matter if it's something that's easy or hard?"

"Yes, you could say that, Laura."

Alex interrupted, "So, if I wholeheartedly want to sleep and goof off all the time, what you're saying is that that's what I should aim for?" He seemed irritated.

"Well, Alex, maybe, maybe not. I wouldn't be able to answer this for you, but I don't think your example here is realistic. I have never met anybody that wholeheartedly wanted to sleep and goof off all the time. And, I have met people that slept and goofed off a lot, and they definitely didn't feel this was effortless. Actually, they felt the exact opposite. And that's my whole point. Because even though it took no physical effort at all to sleep and goof off, those people had all kinds of thoughts and beliefs about how this wasn't what they should be doing and that they should be doing other things instead, which created all kinds of resistance and inner conflict, making it everything but effortless. I think you can all relate to how the easiest tasks sometimes can be the hardest to do and how the hardest ones sometimes don't feel like hard work at all, at least from a mental point of view."

"I totally get your point here, Dr. K," Barbara interrupted. "For me, tidying up my walk-in closet seems like the hardest thing for me to get done, but taking the three-mile run I do three times a week seems like the easiest thing to do. I guess what you would call effortless."

"Yes. In my terms, when doing your three-mile run, there's no inner conflict in you regarding if you should do this or not. And this is specific to you. I know a lot of people that think they ought to run three times a week that never get it done and have all kinds of inner conflict about that."

A lot of people in the group nodded.

"So, what you're going to experience for yourself soon is what this inner conflict is all about. Even though it's an oversimplification, we're going to refer to this conflict like it's between what you feel like doing and what you think or believe you should do. And to achieve our goal of living more effortlessly, you'll learn how to find common ground between what you *feel like* doing, and what you think you *should* do so that you'll move forward without or with less resistance and inner conflict."

"Oh, this should be good!" exclaimed Phil. "That's a battle I'm constantly fighting."

The number of nodding heads told Dr. Krinksted he had their attention. "Well, I'm sure this next stage of incorporating the 3 Minute/3 Step Routine in your life is going to help all of you more than you can even imagine.

Laura signaled that she had a question. "Can I ask a quick question before we go on? When we talked about wanting to sleep and goof off all the time, you said you wouldn't be able to answer this. What did you mean by that?"

"Well, there are many reasons for that, Laura. First of all, wanting to sleep and goof off all the time makes me curious because this fits so well with living in a Performance and Perfection Obsessed Culture. Does *all the time* really mean all the time? Or does it mean sometimes, a lot of the time, some days, every day, or what? Because if you're wise, you'll be spending a fair amount of time relaxing. But in a Performance and Perfection Obsessed Culture, if we're not doing something, working hard, or being effective and productive all the time, we've learned that this is bad, like goofing off. Just look up in any dictionary what the opposite of performing and perfection is. I can tell you that it's not positive things like chill, relax, recharge, or to experience being present.

"But let's say that someone actually does sleep and goof off often. I still wouldn't be able to judge if this is the wise thing for them to do because such a judgment will always be a personal thing. We can all have an opinion about other people's choices and actions, but maybe you know the old proverb to not judge a person until you have walked a mile in their shoes. There are so many factors that need to be taken into account that we might not know about. What is the person's personal and health situation? Did they just finish a long and tough situation in their life? How's their energy level? Are they in some other stressful situation?" Dr. Krinksted took a deep breath.

"All of this leads us to the actual training in this module, because now you're going to experience for yourself what's in conflict inside you when something does not feel effortless. Even though it's an oversimplification to make this practical and applicable for you guys, what you're going to focus on in your training in this module is *what you feel like doing* and *what you think you should be doing.* Here's how you do it. By now, you all know the general information about the 3/3 Routine, so I've made it short."

The doctor shared his screen, showing the new version of the 3/3 Routine made for this topic.

The 3 Minute/3 Step Routine for Aiming for Effortless, Not for Easy

Step 1: Stop and observe

Any time you experience resistance or inner conflict about what you're doing or what to do, stop, take a deep breath through your nose, and observe the tension and sensations in your body and the thoughts that run through your mind. On top of this, in regard to Aim for Effortless, Not for Easy, I want you to observe what you feel like doing at that moment and what your thoughts, your inner voices are saying you should or shouldn't do or should be doing instead.

Step 2: Pause and observe

While you pause for as long as you like, keep observing what's happening in your body and mind, what you feel like doing at the moment, and what your thoughts are saying you should or shouldn't do or should be doing instead.

Again, just observe it all. Don't try to change anything while you're observing, and remember to take some deep breaths while you pause and observe.

Step 3: Continue and observe
When you don't feel like pausing any longer, observe how the tension
and sensations in your body and the thoughts running through your
mind change as you continue your activities, doing what you feel
like doing or what you believe you should be doing or something in
between.

"Okay, that's it for today. Are there any questions before we
break up?"

"Sorry, Dr. K, I need to understand this," said Alex in his old
confrontational tone. "Are you saying that every time I feel like doing
something other than what I think I should do, I'll do your 3/3?"

"Yes, Alex, that's what I'm saying."

"Are you crazy? Do you have any idea how often that happens to
me every single day? It's like I have an inner tyrant constantly telling me
what I should be doing and demanding I do *something* all the time."

"I get it. This feeling of having an inner tyrant like you're describing
is a one-on-one reflection of all the societal pressure we are under in
our unhealthy culture. Many people believe they would almost always
be doing something other than what they think they should be doing
if this pressure wasn't there. But you're going to find out what's really
true for you about this when you start the training. Also, it doesn't
need to take a lot of time to do the 3/3 Routine for this, and you can
always just do steps 1 and 3 if you like.

"So, I sense some of you may be feeling a little skeptical, but are
you willing to give it a try and have a discussion next time about what
happened like we usually do?"

"Well, you've surprised me a few times, Dr. K," said Alex, shaking
his head. "So, I'll give it a go. But I have to tell you I have serious
doubts about this one."

Nobody else had more to say, and Alex was the first one to disappear from the screen.

The Fourth Virtual Meeting

"Hello everybody," said Dr. Krinksted, arriving just at the appointed time. He had purposely opened up for the virtual meeting five minutes early and left his computer, giving the participants time to chat among themselves and get comfortable for the discussion.

"How are you all today? Seems to me there was an interesting conversation going on while I was away from my screen."

"There sure was, Dr. K," said Melanie. "It looks as if we're getting new insights all the time on the different aspects you've been talking about. I'm really excited about what Elinor was telling us because I think I have a little of the same bad habit she's been dealing with. Her experience is definitely going to help me."

"Sounds interesting," replied Dr. Krinksted. "Maybe the group has already heard it, but can you explain it again for me?"

"Sure," said Elinor, smiling. "I had just started, so you haven't missed much. I must say you're right in saying it's simple but not easy. After two months of training your 3/3 Routine, it has finally started to have the effect on my life that you've talked about from the start. I'm now automatically acting more wisely in more aspects of my life, and I feel better about myself than I have for a very long time."

"That's great, Elinor," replied Dr. Krinksted. "Can you give us some examples of what you mean?"

"Sure. You all know that one of the major bad habits I've been working on is spending too much money on things I don't need. That includes time wasted on online shopping, not to mention putting unnecessary pressure on our financial situation.

"Some people call it being a shopaholic, and I completely understand that because it does feel like an addiction. But that's exactly the aspect I've been able to dramatically reduce with your

3/3 Routine. There are times when I might still buy too much, but not nearly as often. For the most part, without really struggling, I just resist the temptation to go on the internet in the first place, which saves me time. Then, when I do go online, I often don't buy anything, and when I do buy something, I feel it's a more conscious choice. And I keep purchases within the limits of what I'm sure we can afford, so my credit cards are looking a lot healthier too. This has made it clear what you mean by true freedom of choice, and I can also clearly see how this whole cycle is driven by a particular sensation in my body."

"Elinor, this is great news. I wonder if you could describe what the sensation you talk about feels like?"

"Yes," said Laura, "I'd love to know that because in my head I'm starting to understand all this and how profound this information is, but in my body, I'm still struggling to identify this feeling we keep talking about."

"I'd be happy to," said Elinor, "but I'm not sure I can. It can't be described with the words we usually use about how we feel. It's more like a kind of restlessness or inner turmoil that's subtle, but somehow extremely annoying. Before I become aware of it, I simply have an urge to do something—like open the computer and jump on my favorite online clothing store. But after using your 3/3 Routine, as soon as I start focusing on what is happening in my body, the annoyance level definitely goes down, and it becomes more tolerable."

"That's a typical experience people have when they learn to consciously face the discomfort in their bodies," said Dr. Krinksted, smiling. "And is this what has made you feel better about yourself lately?"

"Yes, that's part of it. But I now also realize how ashamed I've been deep inside about not being able to control myself and follow through on decisions I've made about reducing my shopping, even though I've tried to give myself all kinds of excuses."

"So, what have your excuses been?"

"I told myself it was because I just loved nice things. But practicing the 3/3 Routine has shown me that this was my nervous system putting this inner dialogue in my head to make me give in. This voice also keeps repeating how I deserve it and life is too short to deny myself this stuff. Of course, I now realize this was my nervous systems trying to make me give in to get rid of the immediate tension.

"As soon as I gave in and bought whatever I had been looking at, I did feel a short relief. But then the inner dialogue changed into two primary themes: One, that this was the last time I'd do it, and I would not give in again; and two, how stupid and weak I was. It became that self-criticism and blame we've worked on together, and honestly, it made me feel like shit. Now that I can better tolerate the discomfort that is the root cause of my actions, I don't have to try to not criticize myself because it just doesn't happen so much anymore. It's like my inner voice is gradually changing from being so overly critical to giving me more normal, healthy feedback on my actions and behavior, and this feels really good . . ."

"Wow, Elinor!" said Dr. Krinksted. "Your story is giving me goose bumps. But I have a feeling you have more to share with us."

"Yes, I do," said Elinor, her face lighting up with a big smile. "As great as this is, it's not the best part. But I'm monopolizing the conversation—maybe someone else wants to speak."

"I hope so," said the doctor. "But please go ahead because I'm sure we're all fascinated to hear your story."

Lots of nodding heads encouraged Elinor to continue. She took a deep breath, as if readying herself to share something that was difficult for her. "Okay," she said. "Let me just quickly say one more thing. I know I don't suffer from OCD, but in some ways, I feel I have always had some of the same traits. For years, I never set the volume on my devices to an odd number, I always avoid stepping on the lines on the sidewalk, and other silly things like that. Nothing huge, but still something that took away a bit of my peace of mind. A couple of weeks ago the idea came to me to try overcoming this with your 3/3 Routine—and it worked! I've been changing this trait by simply confronting the discomfort in me when these things happen, and slowly I've been able to stop following these self-imposed rules. Again, it's an illustration of the true freedom of choice I now feel I have, and it makes a world of difference in how I feel about myself. Okay, I've talked enough—thanks for listening, everybody."

"You're welcome, Elinor. You are very good at describing your experience and your learnings, so I'm sure this will help everybody. Thanks."

Dr. Krinksted noticed that Yan, who hadn't shared anything at any of the meetings yet, had signaled that he would like to speak. "Yan, I think you had your hand up earlier. Did you have something to share?"

"Yes, thanks Dr. K. I'm obviously the oldest of the group, and I haven't shared anything before. But listening to all your amazing experiences has really been helping me. In fact, it has inspired me to try your method and to keep on doing it for much longer than I thought I would. I realize that, at this advanced age, I've probably given up on myself and just accepted my actions—the good, the bad and the ugly. I also realized when we are young, we impose unrealistic expectations on ourselves. I didn't have your words for it, Doc, but everything you've said about our Performance and Perfection Obsessed Culture is exactly what I have experienced. Anyway, for many years I have been drinking more than I should. Not a lot, but definitely more than I would have done if I had true freedom of choice, as you call it. I've tried to change many times, and I got tired of beating myself up."

Dr. Krinksted nodded, and the others were clearly concentrating on Yan's words.

"So, when you said this wasn't about using willpower, you got me curious. I've been doing your 3/3 Routine since you first told us about it, and I can tell you it has given me a whole new perspective—not only on my drinking, but on what being human really means."

"Wow, that's a big concept, Yan. Can you explain what you mean?"

"Well, I guess I was never consciously aware of this before, but I have always wondered why most people—including myself—have certain behaviors that they want to change, but they don't. No matter how sensible or well-educated, everybody seems to have some behavior they know doesn't serve them or anybody else, or maybe even hurts someone or themselves. Some people are like me and drink too much, some are like Rohan with gambling, some can't handle their temper, some lie or exaggerate. It's as if we all have our drug, being addicts to something—maybe the term addict really should be redefined to include us all, just like you've said, Dr. K!"

Although this was the first time he'd really spoken, it was clear that Yan had been taking everything in and had given a great deal of thought to what they were all learning.

"Now I realize that all this is caused by one single and simple thing: our nervous system's attempt to cope with some hard-to-tolerate tension in our bodies. Just that. Period. And I'm happy to tell you that I drink less now without even trying—and enjoy it more when I do.

"I've tried and failed to beat this bad habit so many times that I wanted to be sure your method worked before I shared it with the group, but now I know this will change my life forever. I'm not saying I'll never use alcohol, because if something difficult comes up in my life in the future, I know alcohol is what can help me handle the tension in me. But the difference now is that I am completely confident that when the problem is resolved, I'll just go back to drinking the amounts I want to enjoy instead of using it as self-medication. Use instead of abuse, as you call it.

"Okay, this was longer than I intended, and I'll stop soon, but I just want to say one more thing. I'm not an alcoholic, and I know this wouldn't be the case for real alcoholics, because alcohol has a different intense and specific effect on them. But for me, and those who simply drink a little too much every day, I can personally swear by your 3/3 Routine. Thanks, Dr. K—I'll be forever grateful to you for this."

"Thank you, Yan, and thank you for sharing this. It really is my pleasure, literally speaking. I can't tell you how happy I am that this simple routine I invented has helped you so profoundly. It's helping me a lot to hear all your stories, as they will help me explain the 3/3 Routine in a way that other people will better understand, that will hopefully motivate them to start the same training and experience similar benefits in their lives.

"It's a really subtle thing to figure out if what we're doing is use or abuse. Is there some discomfort in our bodies that we're not aware of that pushes us to take that piece of cake more often than we would like to? Or do we take that piece of cake at the frequency we choose to add pleasure to our life? Are we yelling at our kids for a rational reason, or can't we help it because of some tension in our bodies we have a hard time tolerating?

"Do we have true freedom of choice or not? It's such a subtle thing that it can take quite some time for each of us to figure it out for ourselves. Some of the intolerable sensations in our bodies are so deeply rooted in us that it can take a lifetime to expose, because we have to consciously look for them over and over before we start recognizing them."

Irene, who was usually in listening rather than speaking mode, raised her hand tentatively. "Years ago, I read somewhere that we never really have full freedom of choice because the conditioning we've received throughout our life affects all our choices to some extent, all the time for all our lives. Do you believe that Dr. K?"

"Yes, I totally agree with that, Irene. It's actually intertwined with everything we're talking about around the illusion of free will and what really controls us. Until we bring what's unconscious into consciousness, it will control us without our realizing it. And since it's impossible to ever become conscious of everything in our subconscious, I agree 100 percent with what you've read. The 3 Minute/3 Step Routine is simply one way to bring more of what's unconscious into consciousness, which will remove some of the conditioning, but it will never give us full control."

Seeing several people nodding and others clearly thinking about this, Dr. Krinksted decided it was time to move on.

"Well once again, we've ended up talking about lots of things other than the new aspects you included in your training. But that's only natural, because as you expose and confront more and more of the tension we've been talking about, the better you become at noticing how it pops up in almost every area and aspect of your life. Does anyone have an experience directly connected to our last topic of *Aiming for Effortless, Not for Easy*?"

The 3 Minute/3 Step Routine is simply one way to bring more of what's unconscious into consciousness

---

"Yes, I do," said Diana. "This has been by far the most difficult area for me to consciously face the discomfort in my body using the 3/3 Routine. Or I suppose to be more precise, to do the second step, pausing. I realized there's an almost constant fight inside me between what I feel like doing and what I believe I should do—and the *should* part almost always wins. Or it used to win."

Dr. Krinksted had a curious smile on his face. "Yes, until you do this training, the should part is both extremely strong and mostly hidden from us, which makes it win most of the time. That's how our Performance and Perfection Obsessed Culture negatively affects us so much. But you said *used to* win?"

"Yes, because it has changed. Okay, let me start at the beginning. I always have a ton of stuff on my to-do list. I don't just mean the written list, but the one that's in my head, always focusing on what I think I should be doing. On top of my work, there are always things in the house that could be cleaned or tidied up, and I also want to spend as much quality time with my friends and family as I can.

"After thinking about the discussion in our last session, I realized that situations where I felt torn between what I felt like doing and what I believed I should do were happening almost all the time. I couldn't believe it! And what's more, I realized that out of all the things I could be doing, doing nothing—in the pausing step of your 3/3 Routine—was almost impossible for me to do. Of course, I know that I'm observing the tension in my body, which is not really doing nothing, but that's what it felt like to me. It's like I was at the mercy of an inner tyrant, just like Alex described it, being at the control of his whip. But here's what happened.

"Being a good student, every time I noticed I had an inner conflict, I started the 3/3 Routine, but nine out of ten times I only did steps 1 and 3. But this was enough to start changing things. It was a big discovery for me that the voices telling me what I should do were so dominating that they just won me over with almost no fight.

"But there was another discovery that was important to me. In the past, when I've just done what I felt like doing, my inner voice kept telling me that I was *goofing off* and to behave and do the *right* thing. The inner tyrant that wants me to do the right thing and be there for everybody all the time is the main reason I have a never-ending to-do list, and the reason I often feel so drained and frustrated for not having more time for what I really care about."

Furious head-nodding told Diana others could relate.

"Don't think you're alone in this, Diana," said Alex. "I've fought this battle all my working life, and it's only now with Dr. K's help that I'm starting to beat it."

"Sometimes I think I should write my to-do list on a roll of toilet paper," said Jill, laughing. "That's how long it feels!"

"Well, I'm glad to know it's not just me," replied Diana. "But here's what started happening. It became more clear to me that these voices exaggerated everything—describing all sorts of ridiculous things that could happen—just to scare me into doing something different from what I felt like doing. I began to sit and observe the inner dialogue and the resulting tension—although I'm not sure whether the voices or the tension came first. Anyway, I'm getting better at listening to both sides and gradually making more rational and balanced decisions—and sometimes automatically choosing to do what I feel like instead of what the voices are telling me I should do."

"Yes," said Dr. Krinksted, "that's a good example that even long-term decisions can be just as irrational as the immediate if they're driven by that inner turmoil or restlessness we're all coming to know so well. But Diana, could you say a bit more about what you mean by balanced choices?"

"Well, first of all, I don't know how I could have been so stupid to believe that if I wasn't doing things all the time, I was goofing off. All that running around doing things because I couldn't handle the discomfort in my body was burning me out. So, what I used to think of as goofing off, I now realize is just healthy recharging, as you said."

"Oh, I like that," said Melanie. "I find it helps a lot when I start seeing things for what they really are. I guess that's what Dr. K calls *getting rid of misinterpretations.*"

"Yes, I agree," said Diana. "And I also realized that for me, recharging doesn't always mean doing nothing. Instead, it's doing something I really want to do just because I feel like it. Yes, it uses calories, but it also *gives* me a lot of energy, and that's how it recharges me. Can I give you an example?"

All the faces on Dr. Krinksted's screen nodded.

"Last Sunday, there were quite a few things that needed doing around the house. Then one of my friends texted me to see if I could go for a walk as she needed to talk. Before I started training with your routine, I would have immediately agreed, believing I *should* be there for my friend. But instead of immediately doing that, this time I paused and observed, and, after consciously facing the discomfort in my body when imagining saying no, I realized I felt drained and just wanted to collapse in front of the television.

"But the interesting thing is I also felt like pruning the leaves on some of my plants, something I love to do. On a list of what I felt was most important to do that day, nurturing the plants would be the least important, but I felt like doing it. And that's what I ended up doing. Even though it took me an hour-and-a-half, and it could be described as work, choosing to do what I felt like was the best thing for me. I even had more energy afterwards, so I texted my friend and asked if she still had time to talk. She did, so I ended up doing this as well. This may not sound like a big thing, but for me it was huge."

Irene nodded enthusiastically and interrupted, "That's so interesting, Diana. That's probably why I feel energized after having a cup of tea in front of the television, watching some ridiculous reality show that I'm even somewhat embarrassed to tell people I follow. It's my way of recharging. I never really saw it like that, but now that I do, it's obvious to me that I do feel energized afterwards."

"Yes," said Dr. Krinksted, "that could be your version of the same thing as Diana's gardening. Most of us have habits or hobbies that don't make sense to other people or even ourselves sometimes, for that very reason: it's our way of disconnecting from the hectic modern world and recharging. But it doesn't really work that well if part of us shames ourselves for it."

"I don't want to take up the whole time with my stuff," said Diana. "But I want to make one more point—about the *without lowering your standards* aspect of the last topic. A few months ago, I wouldn't really have had a choice but to say yes to my friend right away because I couldn't have stood the tension that would build up in my body when I felt I wasn't being a true friend by saying no. But in fact, I wouldn't have been there for her 100 percent because I was exhausted. This time, I was able to act more wisely, which ended up taking care of my friend's need as well as my own. I would say this is a much healthier way for me to behave, and I've become quite aware that by tolerating discomfort in my body, I can do more of what's important to me as well as others long term. For me, that's what *without lowering your standards* means. Does that make sense, Dr. K?"

"Yes, it does, Diana, I totally agree. And I have some more thoughts about the *without lowering your standards* aspect. First of all, when we are able to handle whatever sensations show up in our bodies, we become better able to say yes and no in regard to what's really important to us—or not. Until we're able to do that, we can't help but spend some of our precious time and energy on something that's not that important, leaving less time and energy for what's really important. And second, if our nervous system knows that we have a hard time handling the discomfort that arises in our bodies when we experience not reaching the goals we set—consciously or subconsciously—it makes us refrain from setting high goals. We lower the bar, so the risk of not reaching them decreases. I think most people have experienced not daring to set too high goals, right?"

Dr. Krinksted saw a lot of heads nodding.

"And back to your point, Diana. I'm sure we can all relate in some way to what you're describing—being able to be there in a better way for everybody long term—when we're able to include our own needs when choosing to say yes or no to things. I know I can. And this is the perfect bridge for me to move on to our next topic. Before we go on, are there any other questions or comments?"

Encouraged by the earlier support of the group, Yan spoke again. "It's funny how simple all this is, and yet none of us had heard of it before. The world needs this information, and it's just crazy that it's not common knowledge."

"I totally agree, Yan," said Dr. Krinksted. "That's why I've been working persistently on this for so long, even though it was challenging to figure out exactly how to convey it. But I can tell you honestly that the tension I experienced when I imagined *never* getting this information out to the world was much greater than the tension from all the work and ups and downs I have experienced working at it year after year. It has certainly felt draining for long periods of my life, but, at the same time, effortless because there was no inner conflict about whether to continue or not—whether to just go for *easy* and give up on the whole thing. Thank you all for helping me by sharing your experiences."

Everybody smiled at Dr. Krinksted being happy. It was such a win-win situation.

"Can I tell you a little story?" asked Cliff.

"Sure, all examples are welcome as you know."

"When our kids were young, probably six and eight, we were on a day trip to see an old castle. To get there, we had to follow a little path by foot to the top of the hill the castle was built upon, probably about a quarter of a mile long. The whole way on that path the kids complained about having to do that walk to get to the castle."

"Oh, I remember that, Dad," interrupted Melanie, laughing.

"Yes, you did a lot of the complaining, Melanie. Anyway, when we came back to our hotel, we all went to the fitness room. There was a treadmill they wanted to try, so we started it at a low speed they could handle. The kids made up their own little game about how long they could run as a joint effort, and for the next twenty minutes, they took turns on the treadmill, monitoring how far they had gone. I think they made almost two miles—with absolutely no complaints about how hard it was, unlike the little path up to the castle.

"At the time, I thought it was just a funny story and something to kid the girls about, but now I see it relates to the idea of shooting for effortless instead of easy. It was certainly hard work for the girls on that treadmill, but it was effortless because there was no conflict in them between what they felt like doing and any thought about what they should be doing instead."

"That's a great example, Cliff." Dr. Krinksted took a short pause to make the space for more comments.

Hannah started speaking, "I have a friend who's a professional athlete. Her mental coach has told her that it always needs to be what she calls *the amateur* in her that fuels the process. Could this be kind of the same thing as we're talking about here? I mean, as a professional athlete, both the intensity of her training and what she makes her body do and take in competitions are enormous, so I think what her mental coach is pointing to might be what you call *doing it effortlessly*. There needs to be a strong sync between what she feels like doing and what she thinks is the right thing to do. Does this make sense?"

Dr. Krinksted paused for a minute, obviously not having an answer on hand for Hannah's question. "Even though I have never really worked with athletes and heard what you're talking about before . . . yes, this sounds like just a different way of saying the same thing. Thanks for sharing your thoughts on this, Hannah." Dr. Krinksted was happy that Hannah was sharing her thoughts in the group.

After another short pause, he continued, "And now it's time to introduce the new topic for today, which is one of my personal favorites. Most of all, because this will enable you to treat yourself with the same love and kindness most people try to treat everybody else with. This is a huge challenge for most people. You're about to realize how the beliefs we're ingrained with regarding selfishness in our unhealthy culture are twisted and distorted, just like other beliefs we've discussed. The topic I'm talking about I call: *Healthy Selfishness: What It Is and Why It's Best for Everyone.*

CHAPTER 7

Healthy Selfishness:

What It Is and Why It's Best for Everyone

"This builds on what you've already worked on, just upping the ante slightly. I'll jump right to the specific 3 Minute/3 Step Routine for this topic without further introduction, as Diana already touched on it with her story."

Dr. Krinksted shared his screen.

The 3 Minute/3 Step Routine for
Healthy Selfishness

Step 1: Stop and observe
Any time you feel a conflict between taking care of your own wants and needs instead of 1) other people's or 2) what you believe someone else wants of you or 3) what you or other people think is the right thing to do according to the cultural rules, stop, take a deep

---

breath through your nose, and observe the tension and sensations in your body and the thoughts that run through your mind.

Step 2: Pause and observe
While you pause for as long as you like, keep observing what is happening in your body and mind as usual. In regard to Healthy Selfishness, I want you to pay special attention to all your different thoughts and analysis about what to do—your inner dialogue— and how these thoughts and perspectives affect the tension and sensations in your body.

As usual, don't try to change any of it—just observe it. And remember to take some deep breaths while you pause and observe.

Step 3: Continue and observe
When you don't feel like pausing any longer, observe how the tension and sensations in your body and the thoughts running through your mind change as you continue doing what mostly takes care of your own wants and needs, other people's wants and needs, or what follows cultural rules—or something in between.

Dr. Krinksted looked at all the faces on his screen to see if anybody had questions. To his surprise, nobody needed more information to be able to start practicing the 3/3 Routine in this new aspect of their life. Everybody just waved and said goodbye, the screens going dark as everyone logged off.

The Fifth Virtual Meeting

"Morning everybody," said Dr. Krinksted, smiling at all the faces on his screen. "It's been a while since we last met, and I'm anxious to know how you are all doing. Are you finding that exposing and confronting what happens in your body and mind has started to become a habit so that you don't have to remind yourselves of it so much?

"Definitely," said Harini. "I know we've talked a lot about specific changes, but for me, I've found it's just become part of my way of *being* to always have some awareness of what's going on in my body, and in my mind to some degree, like Rohan told us had happened for him some time ago. It has just taken me a little bit longer to get there."

Harini smiled and continued, "Before we all met, I did not have much awareness of any bodily sensations moment to moment—not to mention the ones I was trying to avoid. Now, I'm not so focused on trying to avoid anything really, but being aware of what I tell myself and any sensations that need special attention, then taking all this into account in big and small decisions. It's like part of my daily life now, Dr. K. Then, of course, I have your 3/3 as an additional tool when I am confronted with more serious situations."

Everybody had a smile on their faces, probably not only because of what Harini was reporting resonated with them, but also because she hadn't shared much in the group yet.

"Yes, we've talked a lot about the first benefit of consciously confronting the discomfort in your body—becoming able to tolerate it better and better, without doing anything to stop it—thus giving you a real choice as how to act in matters where you did not really have a choice before. What you're talking about here, Harini, is the other major effect of using the 3 Minute/3 Step Routine: Most of the time, we end up having some automatic awareness of what's happening in our bodies and the thoughts that run through our minds. In addition to this making us feel more grounded, as Jill called it at a previous meeting, listening to ourselves this way will also put us in touch with our own wants and needs, what works for us and what doesn't, to a much higher degree. This constant awareness is necessary for us to make the wisest decisions more of the time. Not listening enough to ourselves is a big issue in our Performance and Perfection Obsessed Culture. Most people I talk to feel they aren't listening enough to themselves, and I can only agree, because we're not. And when we're not, we miss some of the most important data for making decisions. A big part of the reason the 3/3 Routine makes such a huge positive impact in people's lives is because it makes us start listening more to ourselves.

"But let me underline one thing up front that is often misunderstood: Listening to yourself is not the same as following what you're hearing when you listen. There is a typical misconception that we can and have to *trust our gut feeling*. Nothing could be further from the truth. As you've all become aware, many of our gut feelings are based on old misinterpretations and misconceptions that make us act irrationally and can't be trusted. But we have to be able to listen to them so that we can take them into account when making our conscious choices. If we can't and don't, we won't be able to act wisely because we're leaving out some of the most important information when making decisions. In short, you need to listen to your gut, but you can't trust it."

**You need to listen to your gut,
but you can't trust it.**

"That's true, Dr. K," said Harini. "Since I always have more of this awareness now, it's not even an issue whether what I choose to do is for myself or for someone else, because I naturally take both into account and feel I have the freedom of choice to make a conscious and wise decision. Sometimes I choose to say yes to what someone else wants, sometimes what I want myself, and sometimes there's a way to get both. And yes, there's quite often some tension involved, but now I see this as a natural thing and confront it—because I can! Listening to myself is always a good thing because I can then choose to include what I want—or not—in the equation when deciding how to act. It's not saying no to other people but just saying yes to myself."

"Yes, Harini, like we've discussed, being human is not easy all the time. There will continuously be dilemmas of some kinds that will create tension in our bodies again and again." Dr. Krinksted felt like saying more but knew that wouldn't be wise, so he resisted and opened for questions instead.

"That's interesting, Harini," said Diana. "Can you give us some examples of what you mean?"

"Sure, here's one," Harini seemed proud. "Last weekend Rohan and I were visiting some friends, and he wanted to go home kind of early. Before I learned how to have some awareness about what is happening in my body and mind on a moment-to-moment basis, I would have gone along with him automatically because that would be my normal thing to do. But this time, I realized I actually felt like staying longer. As soon as I thought about saying how I felt to Rohan aloud, I felt this massive discomfort, and it increased as I began to speak. But the moment Rohan responded, the discomfort went away, and I felt great! I acknowledged myself for listening to my own wants and expressing them before making a decision. It might sound like a small thing, but this happens regularly now, and I'm getting used to tolerating the discomfort created. I feel good about having the courage it takes to express how I feel."

Dr. Krinksted couldn't resist making a little comment. "On top of ending up with a wiser decision, it made you feel better about yourself as well."

"Exactly," Harini continued, "and it's not being selfish in a bad way because I don't always do what I want necessarily, but I can always take my own needs into account along with what Rohan—or anyone else—wants me to do. I hope that makes sense."

"Yes, it does," said Diana, "and your example makes it clear to me that we need to experience and include this important data when making decisions in our lives.

Rohan nodded his head while listening to the women talk.

Dr. Krinksted smiled. "Also, you're really being more authentic with Rohan, Harini, expressing how you feel and what you'd like. I'll get back to the importance of being who we are when we get to the topic of how to create healthy relationships."

"It also makes perfect sense to me," said Irene. "And I can also share an example from my life. As some of you might remember, I'm a physician. Every Thursday I freelance at a health care center where there's no receptionist. Patients show up five minutes before their appointment that lasts fifteen or thirty minutes, depending on their issue. People sometimes show up late for various reasons, but it's usually just a few minutes. Sometimes, though, someone shows up critically late, which always puts me in a dilemma. Should I refuse to see them that day, telling them they missed their appointment because they're too late? Or should I still see them, putting myself and my other patients way behind schedule for the rest of the day? Having no receptionist adds to the stress because there's nobody to tell the next patients that I'm running late when they arrive.

"About two weeks ago, a patient arrived twenty minutes late for a thirty minute appointment. It was a young mother with a baby, who told me she had been driving around outside for twenty minutes looking for a parking space. I felt that now familiar discomfort in my body—big time! And my thinking went crazy. I felt really sad for her and definitely wanted to help her, and I also knew I would be stressed for the rest of the afternoon if I accepted her because it would inconvenience all the other patients and use up their consultation time to slowly catch up. Whose wants and needs should I take care of? This poor young mother or all the other patients? Or my own desire to not feel that extra stress for the rest of the day? The tension I felt was almost unbearable when trying to make a decision."

"I remember that day, Mom," said Melanie. "You mentioned it when you came home, but I forgot what you ended up doing?"

"I ended up telling the patient that unfortunately she was too late for me to be able to see her that day, and that she needed to make a new appointment."

"So, what happened to your discomfort?"

"Well, this might sound strange, but I felt really good about it quickly. Of course, I felt bad for this poor woman, but I was also happy for the rest of the day as I was able to see every other patient on schedule and not make them wait or be stressed myself. I had never dared to do that before—even though I have been tempted—and I doubt I'd have done it this time either if it weren't for having trained with your 3/3 Routine for quite some time, Dr. K. Because of this training, I was able to make a choice that prevented a lot of tension for me and a lot of other people for the rest of the day. I should probably tell you that the appointment was for the mother, not for the baby, and that in this job, I'm not dealing with any severe or life-threatening situations, so nobody was at risk through my decision."

"That's a great example, Irene," said Dr. Krinksted. "The more severe we believe the consequences are for other people, the stronger the discomfort will be and the less freedom of choice we'll have. That is, until we learn to expose and confront the discomfort directly."

"That was really brave of you to make that decision, honey," said Cliff.

Dr. Krinksted felt how beneficial it was to have this whole family working together on learning and using the 3 Minute/3 Step Routine. "Yes, it was," he agreed. "I'm thrilled to hear that in such a huge dilemma, you were still able to tolerate the discomfort enough to consider everyone's needs, including your own, and not just be hijacked by the primitive parts of your brain. And let me underline that I'm not judging whether the choice you ended up making was wise or not. You're the only person who can be the judge of that, it being your decision.

"I hope you can all see how different this is from the way we typically see the idea of being selfish. In our unhealthy culture, thinking of everybody else before yourself is what's ingrained in us, but when looking more closely, this doesn't necessarily serve anybody long term. Who else has a story for us?"

Alex spoke up, "Yes, I've realized something significant since our last meeting. My previous fear of being selfish has really prevented me from acting in a rational way in so many areas of my life, and in fact, I think it was the reason I lost my temper so much and alienated myself from everybody. I'm sure you all know what I'm talking about."

Everyone remembered the bad-tempered Alex they met on the island, and they smiled and encouraged him to talk about how he had changed.

"Now that I'm aware of the discomfort in my body connected to this fear of being selfish, I end up acting in a way that serves both me and everyone else more often. Now that I dare to give myself the gift of rest and recharging, I become less drained. And less drained means more resourceful, and more resourceful means I don't yell at people anymore. Well, at least a lot less!" Alex smiled.

"I've also noticed that when I'm automatically aware of my own needs and incorporate them in my choices, I don't end up disappointed and blaming other people—and yelling at them—for who they are and what their priorities are."

Dr. Krinksted responded, "That's quite typical of people who work with me, Alex. Fear of being seen as selfish makes us dependent on others to get our needs met, and we end up in what we call the *role of victim*. When we don't take responsibility for our own needs, people have to always tiptoe around us, trying to interpret whether we really mean what we're saying. When we do learn to keep this responsibility, people can help us without having to take care of us or be careful around us."

Alex nodded and continued, "Yes, that's what I've also learned since we last met. I read somewhere that someone called this 'filling up the well by looking after our own needs,' and I think that's a good metaphor. When I take the responsibility to fill up my own well, I don't get drained as often. Now, I have excess energy to help others because I want to, not only because I think I should. I've realized through this routine that without being aware of it, I used to feel people should pay me back in some way when I helped them and have been disappointed when they didn't. But that's not happening as much now due to my deeper understanding of the process—and of myself."

"That's an important lesson for us all," the doctor said with a smile. "I believe taking back the responsibility for our own needs is what it really means to *grow up*. Think about it. A little child will say they are thirsty, expecting an adult will figure out what they want, while an adult is more likely to ask someone to pass them a glass of milk. Or, in fact, just go to the fridge and get it themselves."

"I know exactly what you are both talking about," said Jill. "I've become aware that there are lots of times I would like something but, for whatever reason, I don't say it out loud. I could be waiting for my husband to ask if we should go for a walk—as if he could read my mind! Or sometimes, I just wanted my own space, but I tended to wait until I happened to be alone in the house, instead of retreating to another room or someplace else when I felt like it. It's become so obvious to me how our unhealthy culture has taught me *not* to listen to and take responsibility for my own needs like you just said, Dr. K. I believe this contributed to me and my ex getting a divorce.

"I've noticed how this has begun to change form, and it has happened without me really trying. Just by listening better to myself, being aware of my own urges or energy level, and by being able to consciously face the tension in my body that shows up when I consider my own needs, I've been able to say out loud what I would like instead of expecting other people to figure it out.

"I now see that there's a big difference between *only me* and *also me*. I think *only me* is usually a sign of real selfishness, while *also me* is the healthy approach. It's so true what Harini said earlier, that healthy selfishness is not saying no to other people but also saying yes to yourself."

"I agree, Jill, and I'll be talking more about it later. First, are there any other comments or questions?" Dr. Krinksted saw Rohan raising his hand.

There's a big difference between *only me* and *also me*.

"Yes, I have a quick observation to report," said Rohan. "A few times when we were ready to move to the next aspect of this training, you've talked about *upping the ante*. I think I finally understood what you meant when I was training with your 3/3 around this idea of healthy selfishness."

"I'm glad to hear that, Rohan. Can you explain what you mean?"

"Sure. First, when resisting giving in to a bad habit, doing nothing was creating the tension in our bodies. Then, we had to do something that actually created the tension, and that was much harder for me. Then finally, I not only had to do something that created the tension, but I had to do it in a situation where I felt I might be disappointing other people or letting them down. That was definitely upping the ante, step by step."

"Exactly, Rohan! Our unhealthy culture is making us all comfort-addicts and making us believe that if we're not comfortable all the time, there's something wrong. So, we learn to avoid or try to numb or suppress tension and uncomfortable sensations in our bodies. To succeed in turning this all around, to de-learn and re-learn, we have to start at the easiest end and up the ante from there. For example, if you want to learn how to ski, you don't start on the steepest slopes; you start on a slope that has almost no slope. That's why you started your training around bad habits.

"And you've come so far that you are now using the 3 Minute/3 Step Routine around one of the deepest fears in all human beings, the fear of rejection. Because that's really what we fear when we feel we might disappoint someone—that they will reject us. This is ingrained in us both genetically, as we are social creatures depending on one another to survive, and by being conditioned from an early age by our Performance and Perfection Obsessed Culture not to be selfish. Saying yes to ourselves at the expense of others can be one of the most difficult things for us to learn, even when it's the wise thing to do.

"I could see from the nodding that you could all relate to what Rohan said—that's why sharing stories is one of the best ways to absorb this knowledge. I want to go back for a moment to the idea that taking responsibility for our own wants and needs is best for everyone and the wise thing to do. Are you ready for a bit more theory?"

Everyone nodded.

"There is a spectrum from what we can call _unhealthy unselfishness_ at one end to _unhealthy selfishness_ at the other—with _healthy selfishness_ being the target right in the middle."

"Okay, you lost me there, Dr. K," said Melanie, her raised eyebrows suggesting she didn't get it at all. "Could you explain it a bit more, please?"

"Sure, Melanie, I was about to," Dr. Krinksted smiled.

"_Unhealthy unselfishness_ is when you act as if other people's needs always overshadow your own and, therefore, seek to always help other people meet even their smallest needs before taking care of even your biggest ones. This means you are acting as if you are not as important as other people, and you risk being a pleaser and not taking responsibility for your own needs. Sound familiar?"

People nodded, their expressions suggesting it was only too familiar to them from their past behavior.

"Okay," resumed the doctor. "At the other end, _unhealthy selfishness_ is when you act as if your own needs always overshadow those of other people and, therefore, seek to always have your own needs met, even the smallest ones, before helping other people meet their needs, even the biggest ones. So, you are acting as if you are much more important than other people, and you risk being demanding and not helping—or even stepping on—other people.

"But in the middle is the area where you'll act based on both your own and other people's wants and needs, seeking to incorporate both when consciously and subconsciously prioritizing. With _healthy selfishness,_ you'll be aware of and take responsibility for looking after your own wants and needs while also being aware of, empathic to, and helping others meet their needs. You'll understand, and demonstrate by your behavior, that we are all important and worthy of having our needs met. In my view, this is not only acting wisely but also what growing up really means. In healthy selfishness, you'll be a great friend with yourself and with other people at the same time."

Melanie clapped her hands and laughed. "Brilliant, Dr. K!" she said. "I totally get that, and it's definitely something I want to aspire to as I get better at listening to myself and exposing and confronting what happens in my body using your 3/3 Routine."

"Well, I feel this can be confusing so I'm glad it made sense, Melanie," said Dr. Krinksted with a smile.

"But why do so many of us end up with unhealthy unselfishness in the first place?" asked the always curious Laura.

"Well, that's really interesting, Laura, but it will take a little time to explain."

Irene interrupted. "I think it would help us all to understand this, to really grasp what you're saying here. Personally, I can feel something in me resisting this idea that selfishness can be healthy."

"Well, if you mean this literally, Irene, I'm glad to hear that you're aware of this resistance in your body," Dr. Krinksted said with a wink. "Okay, we have to rewind just a little for me to explain this." The doctor took a deep breath. "So, there are three crucial elements for us to be able to be healthy selfish:

1. The ability to listen to ourselves, to be aware of what happens in our bodies: The sensations, feelings, and thoughts—to know what we want and need ourselves.
2. The ability to tolerate the sensations that arise when making decisions and actions that include our own wants and needs.
3. The understanding of the difference between healthy selfishness, unhealthy selfishness, and unhealthy unselfishness.

"Unfortunately, we typically don't learn either of these while growing up in our Performance and Perfection Obsessed Culture, where most of us learn the exact opposite. That's why all this feels so new and counterintuitive."

"You're definitely right about that," interrupted Irene. "When people ask what I want, it's often like I don't even know. Please continue, Dr. K."

"Well, because there's such a strong belief that selfishness is a bad thing in our unhealthy culture, nobody teaches us the nuances around selfishness that you're learning now. Instead, we learn to always be nice and well-behaved. But that teaches us to be overly aware of what other people around us need or would like from us and that how other people think and feel is more important than what we think and feel ourselves. And we learn this not only as moralization but also from experience. From an early age, most kids are pressured to share their toys with other kids even though they might not really feel like it. They are also encouraged to apologize for something they did, even though they might not feel they did anything wrong, or they might not be sorry at all. And these are just a few examples. Bottom line, we learn to focus on and do what other people expect of us and what makes other people happy rather than listen to and take our own feelings and needs into account.

"Also, having kids is really hard work. For most people, having kids is the best thing ever and part of what gives them a deep sense of fulfilment—and it's still really hard work. Parents with especially small kids are under loads of pressure. So, even if parents did know the difference between healthy and unhealthy selfishness, for most parents there's simply no excess time or energy to stop and help their kids become aware of what is happening in their bodies. It's so much easier short-term for parents—and schools and workplaces—when people are not in touch with what happens in their own bodies and just follow along. This way, it becomes deeply rooted in our nervous system at the subconscious level to simply fit in, and growing up, it stays as the tension you have now become aware of when trying to do the opposite. That is, until we consciously expose this tension and confront it directly."

Laura had a question. "But is this all bad? Don't we have to teach our kids to also fit in?"

"Definitely. Nobody wants their kids to be misbehaving individuals. We all need and want to fit in and be liked. We want this for our kids too. And, as usual, it's a matter of finding a wise balance. In a

Performance and Perfection Obsessed Culture, it's done way too much, like an *obsession,* as the word says. The balance is way off, which leads to unhealthy unselfishness. We teach them that they're in trouble if they don't have their primary focus on what everybody else wants and wants them to do, and then do that.

"And it doesn't end there. Not only are we not taught to be aware of the sensations and feelings in our bodies, we're even taught to de-learn what might have been there in the first place. Indirectly, we teach our kids and each other that what they feel inside is not important.

"We teach our kids to eat when food is ready—instead of when they are hungry. We teach them to keep eating until the plate is empty—instead of stopping when they feel *full.* We teach them to not cry if we adults feel it's not something to cry over—instead of encouraging tears when they are sad. We teach them to go to bed when we feel it's the right time—instead of when they are tired. We teach them to say sorry when we find it appropriate and it's expected—instead of when they feel sorry for what they have done.

"And what do you think is most frustrating for a child: *To notice* how hungry they are—and not get food? *Or to suppress* the sensation of how hungry they are—how they feel—and not get food? Another example—what do you think is most frustrating for a child: *To notice and show* sad feelings and be told they shouldn't be sad? *Or to suppress* those sad feelings and avoid feeling wrong for being sad?"

Dr. Krinksted looked at all the faces on his screen. "Right. So, slowly we ingrain in them to not notice what they feel—to let it stay at the subconscious level. When it gets them in trouble and makes them feel wrong to include what they feel and want in their decisions and actions, what's more natural than learning to not even notice it? Or to suppress it, to do or take one of the mood-changing actions or substances to numb it? Sound familiar?"

"Yes, so it's totally connected to everything you've taught us here from the very start," Laura concluded. "That's how this mutual root cause is created?"

"Right."

"So, we're never really taught to be aware of our own wants and needs—and we're even taught to suppress them."

"Yes. It's easier to bear if we stop noticing what we feel, so we stop noticing," Dr. Krinksted added.

Laura continued, "And we're not taught that it's our responsibility to include our own wants and needs into the equation, when deciding how to act and behave—and we're even taught that it's a selfish thing to do. That's why we all have to learn it as grown-ups."

Irene spoke up, "But wouldn't it take much more time, energy, and resourcefulness from the parents and society to teach this awareness while we're growing up?"

"Yes, short-term, everything flows so much easier when people do everything they can to fit in; that's part of the reason it doesn't happen. That's why we all as grown-ups have to slowly break free from the distorted beliefs of our unhealthy culture. Only when we all do this can we start acting more wisely with our kids and break this vicious cycle.

"Doing this training around the aspect of healthy selfishness will be a long-term game changer not only in your lives—but in your kids' lives as well. But it's one of the most difficult areas, because as soon as you start acting in a healthier selfish way or start helping your kids to do this, I tell you, I promise you, you'll have uncomfortable sensations in your body to use for your training. This will rock the boat like you wouldn't believe. No matter if what you're saying or doing is wiser and healthier and serves more people long term, there's nothing like going against cultural rules and beliefs that can create tension in people and between people.

"So, I advise you to take small steps with this. Don't start with the most difficult things, or you'll risk being too challenged and giving up. And learning to be healthy selfish is way too important to take that risk.

"Okay, let's move on. The headline for the next aspect of your life in which you're going to consciously expose and confront discomfort in your bodies is called: *How to Stop Criticizing Other People: Forgiveness, Part 2.* To state the obvious, this will be a continuation from Chapter 5."

Dr. Krinksted smiled as he continued.

CHAPTER 8

How to Stop Criticizing Other People:
Forgiveness, Part 2

"We already talked about the first area of forgiveness, in which we learned how to forgive ourselves. But, if we are honest, we'll admit there are times when we criticize and guilt-trip other people also.

"And just as you realized, there's nothing wrong with you, even when your actions might not seem that great. There's nothing wrong with other people either—they're also doing the best they can, even when their actions seem to imply the opposite. It's our unhealthy culture that twists what we see as normal and not normal, making us believe that if we don't show up as superhuman all the time, it's because there's something wrong with us or we're not trying hard enough.

"So once again, as Rohan mentioned a moment ago, we're upping the ante. Every time you notice you are blaming or judging someone or feeling upset at something another person did or didn't do . . .well, you know the drill! This is the time to do the 3/3 Routine. Here are the specifics for this aspect of your life."

The doctor shared his screen to show the next version of the 3/3.

The 3 Minute/3 Step Routine to Stop Criticizing Other People

Step 1: Stop and observe
Any time you feel upset or resentful because of something another person did or didn't do, stop, take a deep breath through your nose, and observe the tension and sensations in your body and the thoughts that run through your mind.

Step 2: Pause and observe
While you pause for as long as you like, keep observing what is happening in your body and mind and pay special attention to how the voices in your head are criticizing and blaming other people, and how the sensations in your body and the thoughts in your mind are affecting each other.

And again, just observe—don't try to change anything while you're observing and remember to take some deep breaths while pausing.

Step 3: Continue and observe
When you don't feel like pausing any longer, observe how the tension and sensations in your body and the thoughts running through your mind change as you continue your activity where you left off before starting this specific 3/3 Routine.

"That's it. I look forward to our next meeting. Bye for now."

The Sixth Virtual Meeting

One by one, the screens lit up on Dr. Krinksted's computer as the participants joined the meeting. By this time, they acted more like a group of friends getting together, and the catch-up small talk served to relax everyone and prepare them for the new learning to come.

"Hi again," he said when the last one appeared. "Good to see you all here. I love the energy I feel between you guys even though we are far apart geographically. I have a feeling I'm going to hear some good stories today. Am I right?"

Nods from everyone confirmed his thought.

The first one to speak was Phil, "I have a question. I was wondering how the relationship between criticizing and being hard on ourselves and criticizing and being hard on other people relates to forgiveness? It seems to me that there's quite a leap from stopping criticizing to actual forgiveness. I mean, I can learn to stop criticizing myself for making mistakes, but still make mistakes I should not have made because I should have known better. But forgiving myself or other people seems like accepting that it's okay to make mistakes, and I feel that's a whole different ballgame."

Before the doctor could speak, Phil's wife jumped in, "Can I say something about this, Dr. K?"

"Yes, please do, Elinor."

"I've had the same question in my head, but I think I found the answer while doing your 3/3 training. I definitely feel that not criticizing and forgiveness are different, but the training has resulted in both for me. Since I've become better at tolerating the discomfort in my body, my mind doesn't have to work so hard to prevent me from acting in ways that could create discomfort. This has naturally reduced my self-criticism, just as you said it would.

"But the forgiveness part came from someplace else for me, and I want to say I am forgiving both myself and other people more and more. That's because it has become so crystal clear to me that the notion of free will really is an illusion."

Dr. Krinksted smiled and put up his thumb, expressing his pleasure that one of his key messages was hitting home for Elinor.

Encouraged, she continued, "I have to say that I pretty much always have good intentions, but although I do the best I can, I still end up doing things I shouldn't be doing—like buying something I don't need, or speaking ill of someone when I'm upset, or other things I don't tell people about because I'm ashamed. At least, I used to be ashamed. But because I'm slowly realizing that none of us are completely in control of ourselves, I don't feel so ashamed anymore. I know that sometimes my best doesn't live up to other people's expectations or my own. But at the same time, I also know I'm not in full control. That's what drives the forgiveness part in me.

"It's like I refuse to go through life feeling bad for just being human—because that's what it is really. It's so obvious to me now that our Performance and Perfection Obsessed Culture screws up our view of what we can and can't expect of ourselves, making us all feel that if we're not superhuman all the time in all areas of our lives then there something wrong with us. Now this doesn't mean I refuse all responsibility. I do everything I can to act wisely, and your 3/3 training has made a world of difference. But because I know I've done my best, I experience being less hard on myself. Learning to confront and tolerate the discomfort in my body is directly related to quieting those voices in me that we talked about. I believe forgiving myself comes from the deeper understanding and conscious experience of what it really means to be human. But maybe that's just me."

"No, I pretty much agree with everything you've said, Elinor. I think you've got a good handle on the whole free will illusion and how our Performance and Perfection Obsessed Culture plays out in our lives."

"Can I add something here, Dr. K?" asked Alex.

Dr. Krinksted gestured, inviting him to go on.

"I hope this is okay, because I feel I'm hogging the floor a bit. It's just that I've experienced so much in so many areas of my life due to this training."

"Not at all, Alex. Sharing your experiences helps everybody, and I'm happy to hear that you are getting so much out of what you are learning. Please tell us what you're thinking."

"I also agree with everything you've said, Elinor," said Alex. "And for me, it started with forgiving other people first. I've always tended to blame people and get annoyed when they did something I felt they shouldn't have done—and that happened a lot. But now, when I find myself feeling that way, a new voice has started in my head. It reminds me that they are not completely in control of themselves, just like I'm not. Also, they might simply be practicing healthy selfishness, and their actions could be based, at least partly, on a need they have—which of course, I don't know about or feel or see as clearly as they do. And when I don't have the full picture, I can't really judge their actions."

The doctor smiled and nodded. "Alex, I'm really pleased to see you understand how healthy selfishness also informs other people's actions and that you are taking that into account when judging them."

"Yes, it makes a big difference," said Alex. "After beginning to react this way more automatically—not judging others for their behavior because I know I don't have all the facts—it's sort of another way of saying I forgive them. I'm sure you all noticed how I used to fly off the handle all the time when we were stuck on the island. That was because I was always finding fault with people's actions according to my own rules. But now I don't do that anymore—or at least not so much. I think Barbara would agree."

Barbara nodded and smiled.

Alex continued, "I think what really caused the most change is realizing that no matter how much I want to do my best, I am just human. I have a human nervous system that stops me from being in complete control all the time, and that's the way it will always be. Yes, practicing all we've learned here helps me forgive myself. It's a relief to admit to myself that I'm just human and it's okay—not only admitting it to myself, but saying it out loud to all of you here in this moment."

Alex had obviously finished what he wanted to say, and he received nods and expressions of approval from the group. At that moment, their video chat cut out due to a connection issue. Dr. Krinksted used the time to update his sheet with notes of each participant while the connection was down.

Notes:

Melanie, Melanie's mother, Irene and Melanie's father, Cliff

Melanie

Thirty-one years old.

The enthusiastic young woman who reached out to me and initiated our group meeting. Bought the book because she wants to break a bad habit.

But also wants to better understand how our Performance and Perfection Obsessed Culture messes up her life, and how she can break away from it more. Likes that it's all based on neuroscience.

Bad habit: Has a sweet tooth.

Has started recognizing different sensations related to her cravings for sweets.

Described the sensations she experiences like a restlessness in her body and dryness in her mouth. Even though she still eats more chocolate than she wants to, often she doesn't really struggle with it anymore. She feels like she can now use sweets to bring pleasure in her life without losing control and overindulging in them (use without resulting in overuse or abuse).

Has started noticing that she's observing what's happening in her body even when it's not directly related to an urge to indulge in her bad habit

---

nor when she's worrying or feeling stressed. She calls this being in better contact with herself.

Mentioned that she's experiencing a lot of self-criticism.

Seems like this knowledge is becoming second nature to Melanie.

Irene, Melanie's mother

Showed up to support her daughter. She is a physician, and she wants to make sure what her daughter is into is something sound and rational. As a physician, she's also open to learning something new that might allow her to better help the stressed patients in her clinic.

Nothing new.

Nothing new.

Didn't say much at first, but suddenly showed through her comments and sharing how she has been taking in all the learning and understanding it. She is both using it herself and relating it to what she has read as a physician. Shared a good example from her work and seems interested in understanding everything at the deepest level possible.

And on a personal level, like so many other people, she has so little contact with herself that when people ask what she wants, she very often doesn't know.

Cliff, Melanie's father

Told us that his daughter, Melanie, talked him into joining.

Bad habit: Smoking.

Has tried to quit many times but never succeeded. This is what he's using the 3/3 Routine to work on.

Has already experienced that beating his bad habit using the 3/3 Routine instead of trying to use his willpower works in a totally different manner. Has really started to gain a whole new experience of all the tension and thoughts related to his bad habit of smoking (his craving for nicotine) via the 3/3 Routine. It has become obvious to him that the real reason he smokes is not the pleasure it gives him but the tension and uncomfortable sensations he never noticed before when he reaches out for a cigarette—and how his urge for a cigarette increases in strength when this tension and sensations increase.

He's also catching on to how our Performance and Perfection Obsessed Culture is a real villain in our lives but still something that each of us can break free from once we learn how.

Told us that he can't wait to see how this will help him in more areas of his life when we get to that.

Told us that if there was just one thing he could change in his life it would be to experience less stress and worry.

Showed that he totally understands the difference between Aiming for Effortless, Not for Easy by the story about their kids when they were on vacation.

Alex and Barbara

They are probably in their forties.

Alex

The guy I heard complaining at the reception desk. He said he showed up because he didn't have anything better to do. He generally seems to have a bad temper, and he's very skeptical. He was the one who almost left when I mentioned the notion that free will is an illusion. I think he might be more stressed than he is aware of, and I got the impression that he's not very open to trying to see things in a new way no matter how true or wise they are.

Nothing new.

Alex seems to have changed, and his skepticism has vanished because what he is learning is helping him regarding the stress he is now telling us about. Also realizes how his stress is affecting his wife and their relationship.

Alex has become enthusiastic about what he's learning and how this training is benefitting him in his life. Has realized that what he calls an inner tyrant used to push and stress him to be unselfish the unhealthy way and to never recharge and how all this was part of the reason for his bad temper.

Barbara

Didn't say much. Seemed embarrassed by Alex temper and behavior.

Nothing new.

Has realized how she worries practically all the time —from the smallest things to the worst things she can imagine (she mentioned divorce). Sometimes feels she's going crazy. Her worrying is connected to Alex's temper and behavior, and the risk of creating a bad vibe messes up her life in many ways, not only with Alex. She understands that she needs to learn to tolerate creating bad vibes so she can make wise decisions. Then, she will have time and energy for what's most important in her life.

Barbara seemed happy that what they are learning is changing her husband. And their speaking openly about this created a good connection between them. I noticed that Alex reached out and took Barbara's hand when she spoke about all this.

Also mentioned that she's always criticizing or blaming herself for something.

Nothing new.

Rohan and Harini

They are here with their young daughter.

Rohan

The guy I saw sitting in the lobby flirting with a woman when his wife and daughter entered. He did the introduction of his wife.

Bad habit: Checking his inbox all the time.

Told us of another bad habit—constant phone checking—uses the 3/3 Routine for this.

Rohan seems to be more and more interested and is participating in what he's learning here.

He told us about his challenge with his inability to stop flirting with women. And how he's becoming aware that this is also driven by tension in his body that ends up taking control—and how using the 3/3 Routine when the urge arises makes him better at tolerating discomfort and helps him gain control of this behavior.

Really understands how this mechanism is the root cause of all the behaviors he struggles with. Told us of yet another bad habit that he's been using the 3/3 Routine on with success—gambling. Using the

3/3 Routine has also slowly given him the level of control he wants regarding this behavior.

He feels like what he has learned here and the training has changed his life. Mentioned that he has become used to constantly having some part of his awareness on what happens inside him. The result—time doesn't seem to fly by so quickly for him anymore.

Harini

Didn't say much.

Bad habit: Nail biting. Told us that she hates herself for—and is embarrassed by—her lack of self-control.

Has started noticing something new when doing the 3/3 Routine, but hasn't yet exposed exactly what the tension and uncomfortable sensations related to her nail biting are.

Seems interested in learning more.

Nothing new.

Told us that it has become part of her way of being to always have awareness of what's going on in her body and in her mind to some degree. This gives her the benefits of the 3/3 Routine without having to use it as often.

(Remember Harini's example about leaving the party earlier than Rohan when we get to the topic on Healthy Relationships.)

Diana

The red-haired woman who was the object of Rohan's attentions in the lobby. She is travelling by herself.

Mentioned her inability to relax. The 3/3 Routine has made her aware of the tension and sensations that are connected to this. She uses alcohol to relax and has started using the 3/3 Routine to gain more control of this.

Has discovered that, to some degree, she constantly worries about what people think of her and whether people like her. Even the ones closest to her. Can now connect a lot of saying yes to too much and inability to say no to the tension I point to, which in her case is usually a subtle feeling of having a lump in her throat. Feels it's ridiculous how often she worries for no good reason.

Told us that she feels like what she has learned here is truly profound.

Talked about how her version of an inner tyrant puts her under pressure to always do the right thing and to be there for everybody else all the time, which ends up in a never-ending to-do list. Also has a hard time doing nothing—including the pausing step of the 3/3. All this results in her feeling drained and frustrated for not having time for whom or what she really cares about.

She has realized there's an almost constant fight inside her between what she feels like doing and what she believes she should do. The voices telling her what she should do were so dominating that they usually won her over without much fight. But this has started to change. It has become clearer to her how the voices in her head exaggerate everything to scare her into doing something different than what she feels like doing. She's getting better at listening to both sides and gradually making more rational and balanced decisions. What she used to think of as goofing off, she now sees as healthy recharging.

She's now able to do more of what's important—to herself as well as to others—so she doesn't feel she's lowering her standards.

Regarding Rohan's flirting—it's now become clear to her how he ended up behaving this way because, deep down, he was controlled by his nervous system and not his willpower.

Lastly, she mentioned that it's frightening how time just seems to fly by quickly when we're on autopilot.

Elinor and Phil

The stylish, blond woman and the man that I saw in the dining area that had the discussion about her shopping and his eating habits.

They have a six-year-old girl and a twelve-year-old boy.

At the meeting, I felt tension between them.

Elinor

Introduced both of them.

Seems like she already likes my teachings and the 3/3 Routine.

Nothing new.

Told us that after training with the 3/3 Routine for two months, she's now automatically acting more wisely in more aspects of her life.

Been able to dramatically reduce her shopping habits—understands the notion of true freedom of choice and how not having true freedom of choice is connected to particular sensations in her body, in the form of restlessness or inner turmoil that's pretty subtle, but somehow extremely annoying. Sensations are more tolerable after using the 3/3 Routine to consciously expose and confront this.

Feels she has some OCD traits in the form of irrational self-imposed rules and has used the 3/3 Routine to overcome these also, and it worked for her.

Also, her self-criticism has decreased, and she feels she's much better at forgiving herself when acting unwisely—when just being human.

Told us that she feels better about herself than she has for a very long time.

Phil

Said that Elinor dragged him along to our meeting.

Seems to have also caught interest in what I'm teaching. He mentioned that he's using the 3/3 when the urge for reaching for a bag of potato chips or a second burger shows up.

Has really caught interest now. Told us it has been an eye-opener how often he has tension in his body that he hasn't been aware of before affecting his level of self-control.

Named his bad habit: Eats too much and too often.

Told us that his food cravings give him a short fuse. Can be a bit of a bear at work, and easily loses his temper.

As a side note, Phil told us that they have tried their own version of the 3/3 Routine with their kids.

<u>Laura and Hannah</u>

The young couple.

Laura

The inquisitive one who is doing a master's in psychology.

Has a strong professional interest in everything I teach.

Reaching for a deep understanding of how our nervous system works and the implications of this.

Seems like she's really grasping this mentally, but she still struggles somewhat to actually expose and experience how this happens in her own body and mind, which she's reaching for now.

Hannah

Didn't say much. Was introduced by her fiancée, Laura.

Still hasn't shared or asked anything.

Has started sharing her thoughts.

Nothing new.

Jill

The woman who asked the question about being triggered when her two young daughters tease each other. She's alone with them here on vacation.

It was Jill I had the private talk with. Uses the 3/3 Routine when being triggered when her two young daughters tease each other.

When starting the topic on unnecessary stress and worry, she said that her name was written all over that topic.

Told us a few things this time: She feels ashamed when yelling at her daughters, but also that this yelling has decreased, which makes her feel much better about herself. Feels it's also good for her daughters that she doesn't yell as often and it even makes them tease each other less, which has decreased her stress level.

Under the topic of stress and worry, told us that she's saying yes to more than she has time and energy for because she wants to live up to societal expectations and wants people to like her and not think badly of her.

Finally she also mentioned she's started to feel more grounded since starting this training.

She's really understanding this knowledge on a deeper level. Has started to notice the voices in her head criticizing her. But also, she's automatically more aware of what is happening in her body and in her mind most of the time, even without having to try.

Mentioned having a long to-do list and not listening to and taking responsibility for her own needs.

Yan

The oldest guy who sat in the back. Didn't share anything yet.

Still hasn't shared or asked anything yet.

Nothing new.

Turns out that he's been taking everything in from the very first meeting and has given all the information a great deal of thought.

Bad habit: Says he drinks a little too much every day but is not an alcoholic.

Has been doing the 3/3 Routine from the start and has gotten a whole new perspective on his drinking habit. Really understands the difference between use and abuse. Drinks less now without even trying and enjoy it more when he does.

Said that he has gotten a whole new perspective on what being human really means and that this knowledge and training will change his life forever.

A few minutes later, he saw the faces of each individual pop up on his screen. They were back. Dr. Krinksted was about to speak when he was interrupted by Elinor.

"I don't know what happened but before you move on, Dr. K, I'd like to share something with the group. Is that okay?"

Elinor's husband, Phil, seemed to become more alert, paying close attention to his wife as she began to speak.

"I want to admit to something that only Phil and I know at this point, and I have his total support and agreement to tell you about it now. I didn't say anything before because I didn't want anybody to know—I was ashamed. But having learned all that we have been talking about around forgiveness, I guess that even though I know I did something that really hurt Phil, I have forgiven myself. I want to prove it by saying it out loud to all of you."

She looked a little nervous, but seeing her husband smiling and nodding felt good.

"Go on, Elinor," he said quietly.

"About ten years ago, I had an affair. Even though I knew it was really stupid and something I had sworn to never do, I ended up giving in to the temptation after a relatively long flirtation with a man we both knew. Of course, I realize that I followed the exact same path of losing control as we've all experienced in various contexts now, but, of course, I had no awareness of that at the time. It just seemed like I wasn't getting the attention in our marriage that I needed. I now know it was the inner tension, a sort of restlessness, that made me follow through on the urge that built up in me, but back then I didn't.

"Looking back, I realize that when the uncomfortable sensations grew more and more intolerable, the inner dialogue did everything it could to convince me to give in so I could get rid of this intolerable discomfort. I still remember the voices telling me how I deserved to do this for myself, how I was always letting other people's needs take precedence over my own, how I should just go ahead and do what *I* wanted for once. Of course, when I did give in, all the tension stopped—only to start a new cycle slowly building up until the same thing happened again and again for a period of time.

"I didn't want to feel so weak and stupid, and I couldn't understand why I behaved that way. Of course, like the rest of you in this group, I didn't know about the illusion of free will at that time. Yes, I wish I had acted differently, but I can now forgive myself, knowing that wanting and trying hard to do my best and doing something totally not okay can exist at the same time. I realize that all the self-criticizing doesn't change anything in the past, and it just makes me feel bad for no good reason. And it might even increase the risk of me giving in to other stupid things. The feeling of guilt-tripping myself, when strong enough, risks making the primitive parts of my nervous system hijack me again to do something stupid just to suppress those feelings or make them go away."

Elinor sat back and started looking at all the faces on her screen.

"Wow!" said Dr. Krinksted. "Thanks, Elinor. I'm sure it took courage for you to share that with us. You had to tolerate a lot of tension to be so honest here. I'm so happy you have forgiven yourself for this after all this time. It's a game changer when we truly grasp that we're not wrong for not being in full control of ourselves all the time."

"Can I just squeeze in," said Phil, "that I have also learned to forgive Elinor, after struggling for years to do so. Now I understand what was controlling her. Her affair wasn't really about me, and she didn't act out of what we used to call free will in the situation. I can feel that I forgive her now."

The couple must have been sitting in the same room, each with their own device, because everybody could see how they looked away from their cameras and smiled tenderly to each other. Incorporating the 3 Minute/3 Step Routine in their daily life for so long had clearly lifted a terrible emotional weight from this couple.

Dr. Krinksted was moved by Elinor and Phil's story and wondered if he should underline an important point. Forgiveness is not—as most people believe—something we can do mentally. Forgiveness is something we feel happening in our bodies when we actually forgive, just as Phil expressed. If we can't feel it in our bodies, but feel any kind of resentment instead, we really haven't forgiven the other person. But he kept this to himself, choosing to not risk sharing an insight that might be too much to comprehend by the group at this time.

"Yan," said Dr. Krinksted, "you looked as if you want to add something."

"Yes, but after Elinor's story, it seems like such a small thing."

"No, no, go ahead," said Dr. Krinksted. "Big or small doesn't matter. It's all connected to the same mechanism, so we can learn from it all."

"Well, it's about my temper," said Yan so quietly that the doctor had to turn up the volume on his headset to hear him better.

"I don't really have a bad temper, but in traffic it's like this little devil gets inside me and makes me snarl and shake my fist at other drivers. But since I started this training, something has happened. When something irritates me, like a car cutting me off or beating me to a turn, I notice the tension in my body and a little voice telling me how incredibly stupid this other driver is. But, without really trying, I also experience myself taking a deep breath, and the tension diminishes. I guess you could say in that moment, I automatically forgive the other person. I'm not even aware of all the things going on inside me that cause this forgiveness, but it seems to be the new normal for me. It's kind of weird, but at the same time, it feels really nice."

"That's exactly what's happened to me in a different context," said Cliff. "I'm a big basketball fan, and sometimes when I'm watching a game and the referee makes what I see as a bad call, I get so mad I yell and scream and sometimes walk out of the room!"

"Yes, and it's really annoying when you do that, Dad," said Melanie.

"I know, but have you noticed I'm not doing it so much anymore? That's because of this training. I now understand that the referee can't see what I'm seeing on the television, especially in the slow-motion replay, and I can't see what they're seeing live in the moment, five or ten feet from the play."

Dr. Krinksted grinned, "What you and Yan have illustrated here is worth underlining. For the most part, you won't have to keep doing the 3/3 Routine on the same situations forever, because at some point, it won't be an issue anymore. It's as if when something happens, you automatically face the tension in your body without even thinking about it, right?" Looking around all the screens, he could see the whole group had experienced this, which pleased him. They were really weaving this into their lives!

"Here's why that happens," he continued. "By now you know how our nervous system is always trying to reduce or avoid the discomfort in our bodies that is hard to tolerate, right?"

Heads nodded on all the screens.

"And what's the primary reason we find it hard to tolerate this tension? Anybody?"

"Because," said Jill, "it's subconsciously misinterpreted as something connected to danger, so it needs to be avoided or changed."

"Exactly, Jill. And what happens when we repeatedly expose and confront the tension in our bodies, as we do in the 3/3 Routine?"

"We start tolerating it better, and the misinterpretation stops. Our nervous system learns from experience that although the tension feels extremely bad, it doesn't lead to any real danger, or imply real danger in any way."

"Exactly!" said Dr. Krinksted. "And when the misinterpretation stops, what also stops happening? I know we've already said this, but I'm looking for a specific way of wording it."

"Well," said Jill. "This whole mechanism doesn't even start. The connection to our rational mind is not shut off, and we keep our ability to reason, taking everything into account so we can act more wisely."

"Precisely. So, it's not an issue anymore."

"Yes, that's what I've been noticing too," said Irene. "My bad habits don't take up a lot of my focus anymore. Either I stay in control quite easily, simply tolerating the discomfort of a craving, or I accept that this is just how it is and give in without criticizing myself. As Elinor put it earlier, I've stopped criticizing myself for just being human."

"I can't tell you how happy I am, hearing everything you're all sharing. I love each time I experience one more person having positive change in their life by understanding and integrating this simple, but fundamental knowledge in their lives."

Dr. Krinksted took a few deep breaths and looked around at them all. Each person there could see the effect their learning was having on him as well as on themselves.

"Okay," the doctor said, switching from reflective to active mode. "We're ready to up the ante with our training again. The next area you're going to use the 3/3 Routine is in the area of creating healthy relationships. We have to set aside more time for this topic than we have for the last ones because being able to create and maintain healthy relationships is one of the most important requirements for us human beings to feel truly fulfilled. But don't worry, it's still simple—all you have to do is learn how to *just be yourself.*"

A few faces took on interested expressions as they wondered what Dr. Krinksted meant. The doctor took a deep breath as he started speaking.

CHAPTER 9

How to Create Healthy Relationships
by Just Being Yourself

"Have you ever heard someone say they enjoy spending time with another person because they are able to just be themselves with them? Have you ever said it yourself?"

Lots of heads nodded in response to the doctor's question.

"It's a relief when you're able to just be yourself, feeling you don't have to play a role, and not need to pretend to be something that you're not, isn't it? I know it's just an expression that you might not have given much thought when using it, but it's truer than you can imagine. So, let's take a closer look at what we're saying when we use this expression."

Dr. Krinksted had a big smile on his face, and at this point, everyone knew exactly why. They all knew how he loved when his insight resulted in people being more pleased with themselves and the life they were living. "So, let's dissect what this idea of being able to be ourselves really is and what it's not."

Dr. Krinksted repeated himself, as he so often did, twisting what he was saying only a tiny bit. "Like most of what we've talked about until now, it probably doesn't come to anyone's surprise that *who we are* is not at all what has been ingrained in us. Another thing that might not surprise you is that being yourself is closely related to what happens in your body and mind. Actually, for all practical purposes, who *we are* can be narrowed down to just these components: what happens and has happened in our bodies and the thoughts that are running or have run through our minds, plus, what could be called the *derivatives* of these."

It's a relief when you're able to just be yourself and not need to pretend to be something that you're not.

Dr. Krinksted paused and looked at all the faces on his screen.

Laura raised her hand. "What about our feelings? Aren't they part of who we are?"

"Yes, Laura. We haven't talked about what feelings really are yet, which is needed to see the full picture of who we are. Our feelings are actually a derivative of what happens in our bodies and minds because feelings are the names our culture gives for a combination of these. For example, the feeling that typically includes a lump in our throats and watery eyes and thoughts about something we have lost—we have come to call *sadness.* And the feeling that typically includes pressure in our chest, tension in our shoulders, and thoughts about something happening that we don't feel is okay—we have come to call *anger.* Just as examples."

"What about emotions?" Laura continued.

Dr. Krinksted took a deep breath. "Well, Laura, most people often use feelings and emotions interchangeably, and we will do that here, too, even though they're not quite the same."

"What about our personality? I know I have a bad temper, like you've all experienced," said Alex.

"Right, and our so-called personality and all the other thoughts we typically have about who we are, are also just derivatives of what happens and has happened in our bodies and our thoughts. So, for instance, when you see yourself as bad-tempered, it's because your thoughts are reminding you how you've experienced being upset regularly in your life repeatedly. It's really just a summarization of what is and has been happening in your body and mind since you were born. This is a little technical, which in my experience rarely helps our understanding, so please hear me out. I promise I'll answer all your questions later, if they're still in your head . . . literally speaking." The doctor smiled and everybody smiled back to him, knowing exactly what he meant by this now.

"So, *who we are* is simply what is and has happened in our bodies and the thoughts that are and have been running through our minds. Plus, all the derivatives of this: our feelings, emotions, how we see ourselves, what we would like, and what we have done or wanted to do in our lives, for example.

"So, for all practical purposes being able to be ourselves means:

- Being able to share openly our thoughts at any moment and what we have thought earlier in our lives.
- Being able to share openly our feelings at any moment and what we have felt earlier in our lives.
- Being able to share openly what we would like to do at any moment and what we have done earlier."

"That's how simple it is."

The doctor paused, "And as you'll experience for yourself, when you're able to *just be yourself* in more situations, you'll start feeling even better about yourself and your life—as usual."

Most people smiled at Dr. Krinksted again.

"And here's the opposite; here's what *not* being yourself means:

- Hiding or lying or pretending about what you really think at any moment and have thought earlier in your life.
- Hiding or lying or pretending about what you really feel at any moment and have felt earlier in your life.
- Hiding or lying or pretending about what you really would like to do at any moment and have done earlier."

Dr. Krinksted paused again. "And, as usual, it's simple, but definitely not easy."

Melanie jumped in, "Wow, no wonder so many of us are so screwed up in our Performance and Perfection Obsessed Culture, because first it ingrains in us that if we're not superhuman, there's something wrong with us, making us feel bad—and to avoid feeling bad for being wrong, we learn to put on a show, pretending that we're closer to being superhuman than we actually are."

"Exactly, Melanie! That's why most people cannot really be themselves in most places, if any. Most people are only able to be themselves with close friends or family, when they know the chance of ending up feeling bad about themselves and their lives is extremely low. Some people are never able to truly be themselves with anybody."

"Yes, and it's funny," said Yan, "how performance actually has two meanings. The process of performing a task and the act of playing a role. And what you're pointing to, Melanie, is that our culture makes us obsessed with doing both."

Everybody smiled as Dr. Krinksted continued, "So, using what you have already learned and experienced, why do you think it's so hard for most people to just be themselves?"

For the first time, Laura answered one of Dr. Krinksted's questions instead of posing one. "Is it because what you referred to as *feeling bad about ourselves* is just another word for tension in our bodies and thoughts running through our minds? And if we're able to tolerate only small amounts of tension, we cannot do anything that will create bigger amounts of this other . . . feeling," Laura hesitated. "I know this doesn't sound like a very smart way of phrasing it, but is that right?"

The 3 Minute/3 Step Routine is always about becoming able to; it's never about having to.

"Yes, that's exactly it, and I'm not sure I can phrase it better because there is no specific language for this yet. But what you're pointing to is 100 percent correct. In the process of becoming able to be ourselves more and more, we must become able to tolerate the tension of feeling wrong that accompanies revealing what we think, feel, would like, would like to do, have thought, felt, and so forth, instead of doing and saying what's considered normal, or nice, or doesn't rock the boat. And I don't think I have to tell you the root cause of your ability to just be yourself or not, do I? Would somebody like to tell us?"

As usual, it was Melanie that jumped in. "Our proficiency at consciously facing and tolerating the discomfort and tension in our bodies that being ourselves might create, right?"

"Right, Melanie," said Dr. Krinksted. "It's your ability to consciously face any discomfort that might happen when you are simply being yourself, sharing, or being open about any of the above. We actually got a great example of this when Harini shared an experience a few meetings ago. Remember how much tension she told us it created in her when she had to share with Rohan that she felt like staying longer at their friends' house?"

"Okay, so I can totally see what the training in the context of creating healthy relationships is going to be, and I already feel some tension in my chest and can hear my thoughts trying to talk me out of it," Melanie interjected.

Everyone smiled as Dr. Krinksted continued. "And I want to address something now that I'm pretty sure that little voice in your head is asking. Should we really always share everything with everybody about these three things that makes up who we are? And the answer is: of course not. Like everything you've learned and experienced here, the 3 Minute/3 Step Routine is always about *becoming able to;* it's never about *having to.* Giving you true freedom of choice to act wisely, remember?

"First of all, it would be impossible to share all our feelings, thoughts, and actions with everybody around us all the time because there simply would not be time for it, even if we spoke continuously about them. But more importantly, it would also be irrelevant for most people to know and unwise of you to share your most personal and private stuff with most people you end up being around. No, what this is all about is your *ability* to face the tension that could result from doing it, so that you will be able to *actually* do it when it's the wise thing to do. I wanted to say this up front so that it wouldn't get in the way and prevent you from having the best experience possible in the training you're about to do. And I hope we will hear some input from you all about when you feel it's wise after you've trained.

"So, my friends, this is what you'll include in your training from now on. Every time you're around other people, observe what is happening in your body and in your mind and consciously face any tension you encounter. By now, you might not need to do the 3/3 Routine per say, at least not all the time, because now you're more or less automatically aware of any discomfort and thoughts when they show up. Any questions?

Nobody raised their hand, so Dr. Krinksted continued, "Okay. I can't wait to hear your experiences of this one. Even though healthy relationships are vitally important to us as human beings, most relationships are far from optimal because most people haven't learned to expose and confront the discomfort in their bodies that naturally occurs when interacting with other people. Dysfunctional relationships are not always recognized as such, because dysfunctional has become the norm more than the abnormal. We'll talk more about that next time we meet."

Dysfunctional has become the norm more than the abnormal.

As everybody thought the meeting was over, the doctor quickly continued. "Before you go, though, I have a new and extra routine I want to introduce you to at this stage of your training. I call it *The 1 Minute Reminder.*

"All the training you've done up to now has been what I call *in-context* training. What I mean by in-context is training in the context of when discomfort shows up in specific situations."

Everyone nodded, expressions of concentration on their faces.

"But some of you have already noticed that there's what we could call a spillover effect, meaning that confronting discomfort and thoughts in one situation automatically makes you more likely to notice—and tolerate—discomfort and thoughts in other situations in your life. Why do you think this happens?"

"I can speak to that, Dr. K," said Jill. "As I already told the group at a previous meeting, I've found that I've become automatically more aware of what is happening in my body and in my mind most of the time. So, I'm kind of doing the first and third steps of your 3/3 Routine often without needing to stop and remind myself to do it."

"Right," said Dr. Krinksted. "So, the amount of bodily and mental tension you are aware of and can tolerate in general is increasing, and the amount you can't tolerate is decreasing. Would that be an accurate way of putting it?"

"Yes, that's the way I experience it."

"Good—that's the way I experience it too," said the doctor with a big smile. "And this is what you're going to train more specifically with this extra routine I'm about to give you. I call it an *out-of-context* exercise, which means it's not related to any specific tension or situation. Here's how the 1 Minute Reminder works."

Dr. Krinksted shared his screen so everybody could see his new slide. "First: Decide how often you will use this short reminder and set an alarm as to when to do it. There's no rule about when you should do it—just do it as you like. It might even be at different times on different days—your call."

"Making it effortless," Melanie interjected by reflex.

"Exactly" said Dr. Krinksted.

The 1 Minute Reminder

There are three parts to the 1 Minute Reminder, and before each one, you'll take a deep breath through your nose and repeat the following words to yourself as you breathe out:

1. What is happening in my body and in my mind right now?
2. I don't have to do anything to change what is happening in my body and in my mind right now, because it's okay.
3. All I have to do right now is to experience what is happening in my body and in my mind as fully as possible, without trying to make it change.

"That's all there is to it. You'll just repeat these three sentences for about a minute while breathing in and out. When you do this *out-of-context* 1 Minute Reminder regularly on top of your *in-context* 3 Minute/3 Step Routine, it will multiply the spillover effect you might already be experiencing."

"Oh wow!" exclaimed Melanie. "We can't wait to see how big the spillover effect is. Right, Mom?"

"Right, Mel," said Irene with an indulgent smile at her daughter.

"Okay, are there any questions before we finish?"

"Yes, I have one, Dr. K," said Phil with a grin. "Are you doing all this stuff yourself?"

Several of the group smiled and nodded, and Dr. Krinksted realized how they had probably all been wondering the same thing. He was happy to answer them. "Yes, what I'm teaching you, I do myself and have for many years. And as you're beginning to see for yourselves, after a while it becomes second nature, so I rarely think about it anymore. To some degree, I am aware of what's happening in my body and mind all the time, and I only need to do the structured 3/3 Routine and 1 Minute Reminder when I encounter more profound challenges in my life. Personally, I'm glad to say that after training this way for all these years, I'm now able to be myself most of the time, no matter who I'm with or what the circumstances are.

"I feel I have exposed and confronted most of the tensions that used to keep me from being able to be myself and act wisely and make balanced choices based on true freedom of choice. And you are all witnessing an amazing positive side effect of this: I can now take on big challenges—like trying to write bestselling books and online courses—all because I know I can now tolerate the sensation of what we traditionally call failure in our Performance and Perfection Obsessed Culture. If my nervous system knew I could not handle the discomfort and thoughts connected to—or would have a hard time tolerating—what we call not succeeding, it wouldn't have allowed me the freedom to take on these ambitious goals. It would have put all kinds of thoughts into my head to not follow this mission I'm on."

"So, what you're saying," said Phil with a chuckle, "is that the quality of your challenges has become higher and higher?"

The doctor laughed out loud with delight. "Yes, that's a fantastic way of putting it, Phil. I like that! Challenges are a part of being alive, of being human. We all want and need to take on challenges; it's one of the important ingredients for making us feel fulfilled and giving us the experience of living a full and rich life, which, in my opinion, is what we all yearn for deep inside. Taking on challenges gives us the important experiences of how our competencies and talents contribute to making our own and other people's lives better. And taking on challenges make us grow. On top of all this, life would be pretty boring without challenges, so we'd be crazy to try to eliminate challenges from our lives, even if we could—and we can't!

"Like much of life, it's all about balance. Too many or too big challenges make us stressed. Too few or too small challenges make us bored. What we want is to be able to choose our challenges wisely."

"Yes, just as we have already learned, it's not about lowering our goals—going for easy—it's about finding a wise balance between what we feel like doing and what makes sense for us to do. What seems effortless but not necessarily easy, right?" Laura seemed to understand the simplicity of what Dr. Krinksted was teaching at a deep level now.

Dr. Krinksted nodded. "I share my own example with the challenge I took on many years ago regarding writing my book. The reason I kept working on this was that I wouldn't let it go, even though it felt very hard, very often. It seemed effortless in the sense that I knew and felt I wanted to do this. Although, I can honestly say, that it's been one of the toughest challenges of my life.

"Okay, I'm on a sidetrack again, I'll let you all go now, and look forward to hearing how your relationships fare with the latest training and how the 1 Minute Reminder works for you."

All the screens faded to black.

The Seventh Virtual Meeting

"Hi everybody," said Dr. Krinksted. "I'm happy to see you're all still hanging in, and I'm especially looking forward to hearing your stories today about what happened while training for both Healthy Relationships and your experiences with the 1 Minute Reminder. Who'll start us off?"

The ebullient Melanie raised her hand. "It's just a small thing, and it might have fit better under the topic of Healthy Selfishness, but I didn't realize it at the time, so here goes. A couple of weeks ago, I went to an outdoor music event with three of my girlfriends. We had been hanging out for a couple of hours when I realized I felt hungry— and I realized I had felt hungry for a while without being really aware of it or doing anything about it. At that moment, I also realized how this was a pattern for me. I guess I didn't want to feel I was being a problem or putting people out. So, instead of asking for what I wanted, I would hope that someone else wanted the same thing and would suggest it.

"And yes, Dr. K, I do know what *for some reason* really means here. It's the discomfort I now know I'll get in my body from asking the others to consider putting my needs first, and even just thinking about it! I had never been aware of it before, but of course, it was always there and has always been an obstacle to keep me from asking for what I wanted. But because of all the training I've been doing for so long now, I noticed it this time, and I knew it was discomfort I could handle. So, I was able to act wisely and told my friends I was hungry and asked if they wanted to go for lunch."

"Very nice, Melanie! This is yet another experience of the benefits we all get from raising our awareness of what happens in our bodies and minds in all sorts of aspects of our lives, small and big. Your story may sound like a small thing, but in my opinion, it's huge! All these seemingly small experiences add up to make all the difference in the world for us by slowly making us feel better about ourselves and creating lives that work better for us. In this example, you were healthily selfish. There's nothing unhealthy selfish about telling your friends you are hungry, and it's also a great example of how to create healthy relationships by just being yourself. Do you remember what we said it means to *just be yourself*?"

"Yes, it's being able to share openly what we think, feel, and would like to do when relevant—and that's exactly what I did!"

The doctor turned to the rest of the group, "And can you see how—when Melanie told her friends that she felt like going for lunch because she was hungry—it's related to healthy relationships?"

"I don't know about that, Doc," Jill said. "But I'm reminded of something the marital counselor we saw before our divorce said about treating each other big or small, as she called it. Using those words, when Melanie didn't tell her friends she wanted to eat because of the tension created in her by worrying about what they might think, she was treating her friends small, as if they're also not able to simply express what they felt like doing. In other words, to just be themselves. Does that make sense?"

"It does to me, Jill," said Elinor. "And the thing is, if everybody is waiting for somebody else to say they're hungry, that's definitely not healthy nor wise—and of course they'll all stay hungry. I've been in situations in which I didn't dare say how I felt or ask directly for something, and I realize now that I often ended up trying to manipulate something into happening by planting little seeds, if you know what I mean."

"Yes," added Jill. "And you'll also end up being disappointed that other people are not taking what you want into account—even though you never told them! I find myself regularly falling into this trap, and looking back, it's obvious how I fell into this trap with my ex-husband all the time. It's so easy for me to take on the *victim* role. It's so much easier to be disappointed in other people, thinking they should be able to know what I want, instead of taking responsibility for my own wants and needs because I don't want to risk experiencing the discomfort in my body connected to feeling wrong. Or even acting the martyr—like I'm such a great person for putting other people's needs ahead of my own, instead of realizing and admitting that the real reason is that I don't want to experience the discomfort in my body that's connected to feeling wrong."

Rohan shook his head as he took over and spoke, "Knowing what I know now from all our work on this, I can't get over the fact that we all do stuff that doesn't make sense just to subconsciously avoid having to experience a brief discomfort—big or small—in the moment. It's so obvious to me now how this works."

Everyone on-screen nodded in mutual understanding. Dr. Krinksted was happy, realizing that this group of people were now able to automatically act more wisely and even surprised about why they never did this before.

Alex took up the story, "Yes, and it seems to me that healthy relationships with other people actually start with healthy relationships with ourselves. I mean growing up and taking responsibility for, and including, our own wants and needs and forgiving ourselves for just being human. It seems to me that leads naturally into healthy relationships with others—do you agree, Doc?"

"Yes, yes, and yes!" replied Dr. Krinksted, unable to contain his enthusiasm. "Deep inside, most of us have some doubts about our own self-worth because our culture ingrains in us that we have free will and can achieve anything we want if we just want it badly enough and work hard enough at it. But as you know by now, this isn't true. But because we've been programmed to believe this illusion, deep down we end up feeling inadequate every time we can't live up to the unrealistic goals and standards we set for ourselves and each other. This results in low self-worth, and we compensate for this low self-worth in all sorts of unhealthy ways, all the time. Some of which we've discussed here."

"And," said Jill, "it seems to be clear to all of us, after doing this training, that the best way to solve this problem for ourselves, and other people, is to keep getting better at exposing, confronting, and tolerating the familiar temporary tension that might arise when acting wisely instead of normal, right, Doc?"

"Right, Jill!"

Jill continued, "And with regard to healthy relationships—with ourselves and everyone else—this means not only becoming more aware of what's going on in our bodies and minds and what we feel like doing, but also sharing all this more openly with others. Sharing who we are when we feel it's the wise thing to do. Sharing what we think and what we feel like doing. I can see how this will increase the intimacy in many of my relationships, which is something I would definitely like. Oh boy, I'm so excited about all this, and the more I learn about it the more excited I am!" Jill sat back in her chair with a content look on her face.

"Yes, and intimacy with yourself. Experiencing what's happening in our bodies, including the inner dialogue in our minds, is another way of describing we're listening better to ourselves and getting to know ourselves better. And while we're on this subject," the doctor said with a big smile, "there's one more crucial relationship that will become healthier over time. I hope you're ready for this one."

He looked at all the screens and saw people waiting for this new revelation.

"It's our relationship with life itself!"

As he had expected, the expressions had now changed to curiosity, so he hurried to continue, "I can see from your faces that you're wondering what the heck I'm talking about. Well, most of us learn that we can and need to figure out and conquer life. To some extent, most people live like life is a battle they should be able to win. Our culture ingrains in us that if we want something badly enough and try hard enough, we can do anything we want and shape the world the way we want it. But as we've already experienced in our time together, we're not only *not* in control of ourselves, we're also *not* in control over what happens in many—even the most crucial—circumstances of life. No matter if we do our best and try as hard as we can, we'll never be able to make everything perfect or be able to reach unrealistic goals. We're not gods or superhuman.

"If we ever want to have a chance of feeling truly fulfilled in life, we'll have to let go of the belief that if we want something badly enough and try hard enough, we can make anything happen. It doesn't work that way. We're just human. Life is not a battle we are able to win. And fighting a battle we can't win but falsely think we should be able to win is what creates so many of the challenges and problems we face.

"One of the most amazing benefits you'll receive from this training is that your relationship with life itself will be healthier. Because you'll finally realize what it really means to be a human being."

Dr. Krinksted stopped speaking and gave his head a little shake. And then he continued, "But I've gone off on a tangent because I find it so exciting! Let's get back to the topic of creating healthy relationships by just being ourselves."

Laura raised her hand. "Can you give an example of when it's not wise to be ourselves?"

"Yes, and we have to make a distinction first. My examples will be related to ordinary lives in our part of the world because I can think of many situations around the world in which someone must conceal who they really are to avoid putting their life in danger. But in ordinary lives like ours, it's not really about not *being* ourselves but more about not necessarily *showing* or sharing all of ourselves in all situations. There's a difference between being private and being personal. In a work relationship, it might not be relevant to share private information and opinions, or at least not all of them. The same goes for new or superficial relationships. Like we've already discussed, it's all about *being able to* be yourself, so that you have true freedom of choice to act wisely. If you want intimate relationships with people close to you, you'll need to be able to share what you think and feel to a large extent. On the other hand, in work relationships it might be irrelevant or even create unnecessary problems if you share too much private stuff. Does that answer your question, Laura?"

Laura nodded.

"Another important benefit of just being yourself that is often overlooked is you're actually inviting other people to be themselves too. When you take responsibility for your own wants and needs, you leave an empty space, a vacuum, for other people to step into and take responsibility for theirs too. Treating others *big*, as Jill's therapist described it. When Melanie spoke up and told her friends she was hungry and wanted to eat, her friends were invited to express what they wanted too, right?"

"Yes," said Melanie, "that's exactly what happened. Two of them seemed relieved that they could now say they wanted to eat too. But something else happened then. Our other friend hesitated, saying she had thought we were going over to hear the band that was about to start their set. There was a moment's silence as we all considered the situation. I immediately felt the discomfort in me and noticed how my mind went through all kinds of scenarios of what to say so that I could have lunch now, or wondering if I should just say okay to avoid more discomfort in me and between us.

"It seems crazy, but now I'm so aware of all this going on. Before, I would have gotten all bent out of shape trying to not rock the boat and ended up letting myself down—probably getting a headache because that's what usually happens when I forget to drink or eat enough during the day."

"So, what did you end up doing, Mel?" asked Cliff.

"Well, I ended up not having to do anything, Dad, because one of the other girls spoke up and said she wanted to eat first and then go and hear the last part of that concert, and that's what we did. And that fits what you said, Dr. K, because I do believe if I hadn't spoken up first, she wouldn't have either—and we'd all have ended up enjoying the music less because we were hungry! I know this is a small thing in the grand scheme of things, but for me it was *amazing* because it was a new part of me emerging."

"Right, becoming more aware of what's happening *in* you is crucial. Listening more to yourself, so to speak, will change everything for you because then you can't help but be aware of how it all plays out in your own life and other people's lives all the time. As I've said before, this awareness in itself will make the changes happen automatically without a lot of struggle. Can you see how incorporating this simple practice into your life has a ripple effect that not only improves your own self-esteem, life, and relationships, but will also positively affect other people's lives too?"

"Yes, I can see that, Doc," said Cliff. "And I can see how it works the other way around as well. What we're actually doing when we're not able to be ourselves and be healthily selfish is playing a role, withholding and ultimately lying—and that keeps us all in a *Catch 22* loop."

"I agree," said Dr. Krinksted. "We learn to pretend and conceal what we really think and feel, which means we have to use manipulation to get what we want. And when people around us don't take responsibility for our wants and needs, we feel disappointed. So, we keep perpetuating these dysfunctional relationships that are not always recognized as such, because dysfunctional has become the norm. Like we have talked about before: most of us grow up and live in what I call normal dysfunctional families because dysfunctional has become more the norm than the abnormal."

"And part of the problem," Cliff continued, "is the false notion in our culture that we do this to be good people, to be good to each other, by not saying something that might make people feel bad. But it's not that. It's really to keep from rocking the boat in the moment, protecting ourselves from having to experience our version of tension that can end up almost intolerable to us. Right?"

"Exactly, Cliff. We're back to the same root cause you're all familiar with by now, and in this case, the consequence is that we end up alienated from each other."

Cliff sat up straighter in his chair, becoming more animated as he continued talking. "So, are you saying we shouldn't care about offending and hurting other people's feelings?"

"No, that's not what I'm saying at all. Once again, we need to include some nuances for this to make sense. Of course, we have to take into account the fact that people might be offended or feeling hurt when we are just being ourselves—sharing our thoughts and feelings about something—especially something concerning them.

But note that I say *take into account*. Because being obsessed with not offending or avoiding making others feel hurt, like our culture ingrains in us, is totally different. Every time we hide what we really feel and think, we're alienating each other, which isn't healthy. To create the deep and intimate relationships that we all need, we must share our thoughts and feelings regularly. Of course, we should always have one eye watching for the risk of offending and hurting other people's feelings, and there are definitely places and situations where it's wise to let this focus weigh heavily. But we need *to be able to* be ourselves, to share what we really think and feel—even when it might hurt or offend someone—to create the healthy relationships that play such an enormous role when it comes to feeling fulfilled in life."

While Dr. Krinksted took a deep breath, Cliff took over again, "So, what you're indirectly pointing to as well is that until we learn to expose and tolerate more of what is happening in our bodies and minds so we can act healthier and more balanced more of the time—we're really part of the problem."

"Yes, and that's another thing I love about teaching this. Even if you're only doing this to make your own life better, it will always have a ripple effect that helps others, whether you intend it or not."

"So, we're either part of the problem or part of the solution," said Cliff thoughtfully.

Dr. Krinksted looked like he was trying hard to decide how to respond to this. "Yes, I'm so sorry, but that's true. I generally don't stress this, because I don't want to risk making anybody feel obliged to live their life the way I suggest, or to have it on their to-do list of moral obligations. We're under enough pressure in our culture as it is, and I don't want to add to it. And yes, as you said, Cliff: *you're either part of the problem or part of the solution.* That's why I hope you've all become so fond of the 3 Minute/3 Step training and 1 Minute Reminder that you can't help but continue using them in your lives. I like things to be effortless, you know. I would love to see you all become role models for fighting our unhealthy culture, and I would love it to be effortless for you."

Dr. Krinksted couldn't stop himself now. "If we do it together, we can create a new normal where we prioritize what's most important in life instead of feeling like we're in a rat race, never able to live up to everything that's expected of us while time seems to fly by too quickly. To succeed, we need to create a movement of people that slowly but surely break free from our Performance and Perfection Obsessed Culture. Isn't it fantastic, that even if our primary goal with this training is the value we create in our own lives, we will still transform from being part of the problem to being part of the solution that will benefit everybody?"

We will transform from being part of the problem to being part of the solution.

Dr. Krinksted smiled, and everyone else nodded, realizing they had just heard him explain exactly why he couldn't help but work hard—but effortlessly—with this.

After a short break, Dr. Krinksted continued, "What I just shared was meant for our last meeting, and I want to go back for a moment to Melanie's story. Did you all notice what her friend said?"

"Something about thinking we were on our way over to hear a band?"

"That's right. And what do you think of that in regards to healthy relationships?"

Melanie jumped in, speaking quickly as she realized what Dr. Krinksted meant. "Well, in one way, we could say she's simply sharing her thoughts. But reflecting on my own behaviors, I think it's more likely that this was her way of trying to make us do what she wanted—to go and listen to the band before having lunch—but without saying it directly."

"I agree. The risk of creating discomfort is often less when we don't state explicitly how we feel or what we want. She could have said she preferred to go and listen before having lunch, and even asking if you could do that, which would have been asking for what she wanted. What she said could be manipulative—and if so, probably subconsciously—because it was pointing in a direction but not really showing who she was, because that comes with the risk of feeling wrong."

"But, Dr. K," interrupted Jill, "wasn't she just sharing her thoughts?"

"Yes, you could say that also. It's really subtle, and we can only guess, because of course, none of us knows what was going on in Melanie's friend's head. But let's just use the situation for our discussion here to delve more into this subject. What do you all think?"

"It might have been an automatic response," said Elinor. "But I think it's typical for most of us to have a hard time saying exactly what we want. I think there's a deeper reason than an automatic response."

"And what do you think that could be?" Dr. Krinksted asked.

"Well for me, it would be fear of rejection, as we've talked about before. When I state my wants, and someone else wants something different, I often feel wrong and rejected. And I hate that. I'd do anything to not feel wrong or rejected."

"Yes, and you're not alone, Elinor. The existential fear of rejection is deeply rooted in the human nervous system. We use the expression that it's *in our genes*, but it's really in our nervous system, the remnants of how we could have died if we were rejected by the group many generations back. At its heart, it's the fear of death. So, the reason a simple discomfort in our bodies can make us do seemingly irrational things is that our nervous system misinterprets the discomfort as a threat to our *survival*. And if dying is the alternative to taking an unwise action, any unwise action will be rational no matter what the long-term consequences might be if you know the alternative is death."

"Which is why it's so important to consciously confront the discomfort—because that's how the misinterpretation will stop, right? That's how the false beliefs that are ingrained in us will be replaced with what's really true," Elinor replied.

"Exactly," said Dr. Krinksted with a smile.

But Elinor wasn't totally clear yet. She asked another question. "So, how is this different from the concept of facing our fears?"

"Well, it really isn't different, Elinor. It's just facing your fears at the root, which makes it so much more effective. This inability to tolerate discomfort in our bodies lies at the root of all fears because our nervous system interprets it as being able to lead to death."

"So, it's the combination of our Performance and Perfection Obsessed Culture and our human nervous system that's so poisonous?" Laura always wanted to dig all the way to the bottom of things.

"Yes, Laura, we cannot change how our nervous systems are wired, but we can correct the misinterpretations and break free from our unhealthy culture. And just like weeding your garden, when we attack at the roots, we get better results and can sometimes actually solve the problem for good."

Looking a little worried, Hannah spoke up. "I wasn't going to share this, but I feel I want to now. I have this thing about the small dark hairs on my face and on my arms. It's on my whole body, but it's the hair on my face and arms that mostly causes the problem because that's where it's visible. I have no idea how this started, or why I have such a hard time with people being able to see my body hair, but I've always felt that way. Most days before I go out, I take a lot of time to remove or hide this body hair.

"The thing is, even though the hair is dark like the hair on my head, it's not extreme in any way. I always figured I was ashamed of my body hair, which could be true, but now I realize that it's probably driven by a deeper fear of rejection. I feel panic just thinking about how you would all react if you could see my body hair right now. It makes sense to me now that the mechanism and root cause of this are the same as for all the other things we've talked about."

"Thanks for sharing this, Hannah," said the doctor with a gentle smile. "I can imagine this isn't easy for you to talk about."

"No, it sure isn't."

"So how do you feel right now?"

"I'm sweating in the palms of my hands, and I can feel my heart beating, but I actually feel kind of relieved too. I suppose I was subconsciously predicting that you would all reject me, but I am experiencing that you didn't. I sense understanding and compassion from you guys as I look at your faces. Maybe even admiration—or at least that's the story I notice I'm telling myself now! It's the total opposite of what I was afraid of before I told you this." Hannah felt warmth in her body as the group smiled and nodded.

"Yes, we're all telling ourselves stories all the time, and they're never 100 percent true—and often they're the exact opposite. Once again, you've experienced another version of what we've been talking about from the beginning. In telling us about this fear, Hannah took an action that would create discomfort that would be hard for her to tolerate. But you all know by now that our nervous systems typically over-exaggerate how dangerous such discomfort really is when it happens. Under the right circumstances, it's such a relief to say it openly and experience how other people don't react the way we feared. Keeping all this stuff in our own heads is so poisonous."

Heads nodded on all the screens, and Dr. Krinksted carried on. "Actually, when I was younger, I had a similar feeling about my nose! Whenever I sensed someone looking at me closely, I thought it was because they noticed that my nose was really big. Of course, most teenagers have this type of hang-up about something, but for some people, it lasts beyond the teenage years.

"As a physician, it seems to me that most common psychological problems are just extreme versions of normal character traits," said Irene. "It's normal to be sad sometimes and have low energy, but when it becomes extreme, we call it depression. We see it as normal to be a little anxious when we have to meet new people, but if it's too much or too often, we call it social anxiety."

"Yes," said Diana. "I don't think I have OCD, but like Elinor, I definitely have some of the characteristics of OCD. Sometimes I'm more affected by them than other times, and I've noticed they haven't been too bad since I started this training. And what I just realized is that these characteristics are another example of something normal that ends up getting a name when it becomes extreme.

"I think most people want or need things to be a certain way in the normal course of events. For example, one of my friends always checks an extra time when she leaves the house to make sure the door is locked. My mum can't resist straightening the pillows on the couch. Maybe these could be seen as mild forms of OCD. But everybody talks about OCD symptoms as if they weren't connected in any way to normal behavior."

"Yes, I know what you mean," said Dr. Krinksted. "And I agree with you to a large extent. Often, when such behaviors start interfering with what we call *living a normal life*, we give them a name."

Everyone nodded, gradually realizing how much the mechanism they had learned about in this training affected so many areas of their lives.

"Wow, this makes total sense to me," said Hannah. "My issue about my hair varies a lot, depending on how other aspects of my life are going. If things are okay, it's not too bad. But if I'm generally challenged, then the hair thing feels worse. Is there a reason for that, Dr. K?"

"Yes, it's because the spillover effect we've talked about works both ways. We can typically take a certain total amount of discomfort. So, if there's not a lot coming from other areas, we can tolerate more in our problem areas. But if there's a lot of tension in other areas, then there's not much capacity left to tolerate the tension in our problem areas."

At this point, Yan spoke up. Since he hadn't said much, the group immediately paid close attention to what he was saying. "I can relate to that. Years ago, I was a smoker, and like most smokers, I tried to quit numerous times. I did eventually quit, but started again twice. The first time I started again was when I lost my job, and the second was when I almost got divorced. The extra stress of these two situations sent me back to the comfort of my cigarettes. Of course, I hadn't heard any of the stuff we're talking about here at that time, but looking back at it now, it's obvious the cigarettes were soothing the tension that those situations multiplied in me, and they helped me relax. But even though I smoked a lot during these two times, I was able to quit again when the crises passed, and I never started again."

Jill leaned towards her screen and spoke up, "Isn't that what happens when we say someone has a short fuse? I mean, it's like when some of my fuse has been used up with discomfort created in other areas of my life, there's only a short part left over when my kids start teasing each other. I feel as if that's what happens when I lose my temper with my kids. Could that be right?"

Dr. Krinksted showed a thumbs-up. "Yes, you've got it, Jill! Seeing how you're all taking this in makes me feel all these years of persevering with this work has been worthwhile."

"Well, I'm certainly glad you persevered, Dr. K," said Melanie brightly. "It's pretty obvious you've helped every one of us, so I think your book must have helped thousands of people all over the world."

Dr. Krinksted nodded his thanks with a smile.

"There's something else I've realized since we last met, and I'd like to share it with the group," said Rohan. "I can now see how I've made it impossible to experience feeling really loved when I haven't dared to just be myself."

"That's interesting, Rohan," said the doctor. "Please say a little bit more."

"Okay, as I gradually feel more able to be myself—even though I certainly feel tension in the room and in myself when I do—I also notice I have generally started to feel more loved. It's suddenly obvious to me that only when I'm able to just be myself, as you call it, will I be able to experience unconditional love. Because when I know I'm pretending, I will never experience people loving me unconditionally, because I will keep believing that if they knew who I really was they wouldn't love me. I mean, how can I feel people love me for who I really am when I don't show them who I really am? I don't know how to describe it. Does any of this make sense?"

"Absolutely," said Dr. Krinksted, "and I'm glad you brought this up because I believe this might be one of the most valuable results of being able to just be who we are. And you're right, if you know deep down that you're not showing who you really are—that you're playing a *role*—you also know that it's the *role* they love. So, this love is conditional on you doing what you think they want you to do and being who you think they want you to be. Not until you show up as the real you, and they still love you, will you ever feel their love is unconditional."

Having spoken emotionally about this, Dr. Krinksted closed his eyes momentarily and took a deep breath before continuing, "I want to go back for a moment to what we called the spillover effect, and the 1 Minute Reminder I gave you last time we met. Does anyone want to quickly share their experience with this new reminder routine? I say quickly because we've already been talking for quite a while, and I still want to introduce you to the next—and last—topic."

"Yes, I do," said Phil. "I must admit I've been struggling with all this. Even though I could understand and experience what you were telling us, I felt that when I was doing your 3/3 Routine, I always gave in way too soon, so I felt as if I wasn't learning. In fact, I envied everyone else because they seemed to be having more success with all this than I was."

"So, you didn't experience a change in your behavior?" Dr. Krinksted asked.

"Well, no, that's not totally true. It has changed, but much more slowly than I wanted and, as I say, more slowly than I felt everyone else's had. Maybe that's part of the problem in our Performance and Perfection Obsessed Culture; we always compare ourselves with everybody else. But here's what I wanted to share.

"Since our last meeting, I set an alarm every hour and did your 1 Minute Reminder. It wasn't easy because, of course, sometimes the shop was busy, and I had customers to attend to. But because it only took one minute each time, I popped in back and did it—sometimes even while I was fetching something for a customer."

That brought a chuckle from several of the group, including Phil's wife, Elinor.

"But this is what caused the shift for me. First of all, I became aware that I'm pretty tense most of the time, much more than I realized. And here's what also happened. Doing your 1 Minute Reminder every hour, breathing and reminding myself that the discomfort in my body was okay, made me aware of the tension and how I really was able to tolerate it. I think the trick for me was doing this before something triggered such a strong discomfort that I wasn't able to pause for long at all. I can't really explain it."

"No, I totally get it, Phil," said Rohan. "When the in-context training is too difficult, you won't get so much from it. Using Dr. K's previous example, it's like if you were learning to ski and you started on the steepest slope—you'd keep falling and not learn anything. You have to start with steps that are big enough to learn but not so big that you fall before you even learn anything."

"Exactly," said Phil. "That's what I was trying to say."

The short general discussion that ensued showed that everyone had benefited from the 1 Minute Reminder in their own ways.

Dr. Krinksted continued, "Okay, let's stop there now, as I do want to introduce you to the next topic in our course, and then we can bring an end to this meeting—which has already lasted beyond our usual hour.

"I'm super exited to tell you about the next topic, because no matter how much what you've experienced up until now has made a positive impact in your lives, it's nothing compared to what we're going to focus on now. I'm going to tell you about what I consider the ultimate life benefit of this knowledge and training."

CHAPTER 10

The Ultimate Life Benefit:

How to Experience a Full and Rich Life

D r. Krinksted could sense an excitement within the group, which was not a surprise because they now knew they were coming to the end of their time together and that something special was coming up next.

"Right, so you're about to take the final step and harvest what I call *The Ultimate Life Benefit* of what you've learned here. Ready?"

"You bet!"

"Can't wait, Dr. K."

"Okay, up until now, I've had you focus on something that creates what most people would consider extremely positive changes in their life. Most of you have experienced how this has made you feel better about yourself and your life in one or more specific ways, right?"

"Sure."

"Absolutely."

"What I'm about to tell you now might sound contradictory to all that has gone before, but that's why you will once again have to experience it for yourself in order to understand the full impact.

"As usual, we'll get into it in more detail next time we meet, but for now, let me tell you what you'll add to your training so that you can start harvesting this marvelous benefit for yourself."

"Wow, this sounds exciting," said Melanie.

Everyone smiled, now being used to Melanie's overenthusiastic contributions to the discussions.

"Yes, it is Melanie. If you haven't experienced this knowledge and training as life-changing yet, I hope this segment will do it. I realize from our last discussion that some of you have already been doing what I'm going to teach you now without even realizing it or trying to do it. Here's what it is.

We all deserve to feel good about ourselves and the lives we live even when things are not perfect.

"As well as doing the 1 Minute Reminder at a set time and the 3 Minute/3 Step Routine when experiencing tension, I now want you to also start training your ability to consciously have some awareness of what's going on in your body and mind at all times. I know many of you have already experienced this happening without even focusing on it, and now I want you to make a point of training this specifically. It's not really possible to make a structured routine for this training, so all I want you to do is to notice what you're noticing whenever it comes into your head naturally. That's it, really. Any questions or comments?"

Jill had a comment. "Yes, I'm one of those for whom this is already happening, and as I've mentioned before, as a result, I'm feeling much more grounded and present with myself. I'm looking forward to seeing how far I can go when I actually make this a focus point because it has felt really good so far."

Everyone could see how happy Jill was when sharing her experience and thoughts with everybody.

Dr. Krinksted continued, "Yes, and I'm happy to know that several of you have felt this. It's at this point that many people realize that something more profound is happening on top of improving various aspects of their lives and their self-esteem by making more wise choices and being able to follow through on them. And this benefit that's more profound than all the other benefits you have experienced by now is what I call the ultimate life benefit.

"In fact, this ultimate life benefit was really what drove me to use so many years of my life to write my book. We all deserve to feel good about ourselves and the lives we live even when things are not perfect. But more than that, every human being on earth deserves to feel that they are living a full and rich life every day. Life is simply too short to be wasted letting time fly by without experiencing as much as possible every single moment.

"Okay, I'm getting ahead of myself again—I can't wait to hear your stories and experiences at the next meeting. See you all then."

The Eighth Virtual Meeting

As usual, Dr. Krinksted felt intrigued as the faces appeared on his screen. He knew there would be great stories, and he would feel their excitement as they shared the benefits his training had brought to their lives since they met on the infamous island holiday.

"Hi everybody," he said. "Great to see you all again. Okay, let's hear what has happened for you all since we last met."

Yan spoke up, his expression more serious than usual. "Can I start first, Dr. K? Because today I have something I really want to share."

"Of course, Yan. Are you okay?"

Holding back his tears with difficulty, Yan shared his news. "Yes, I'm okay, but my worst nightmare happened last week. My grown-up daughter, Marie, was . . ." He stopped speaking, drawing little gasps as he began to cry. "She was diagnosed with cancer."

"Oh no, I'm so sorry to hear that," said the doctor. "How are you?"

Yan dabbed his eyes with a tissue. "Well, she's not through all the tests yet, but it doesn't look good. She will probably need both surgery and chemotherapy. It's breast cancer."

"I'm so sorry, Yan," said Dr. Krinksted. "And how are *you*?"

"It's really tough. I cry a lot when I'm alone, and when I'm with my wife, we both cry sometimes. I try to be strong when I'm with Marie though. She's got enough to contend with without having to worry about us on top of it."

"I understand. Is there anything we can do for you?"

Yan wiped his eyes again. "No, thanks Doc, I just needed to say it out loud so that I could stay present today. I'm really happy to be here with all of you. I haven't told many people yet, and some of the people I have told have reacted in a way that doesn't really help me. I want to be able to just talk about it and get it out, but it doesn't work that way with most people. It's like everybody wants to try to make me feel better, telling me to not worry until we know how bad it is and stay positive and all that stuff. But I'm just so afraid and sad right now."

"Of course you are, Yan. The problem is that in our Performance and Perfection Obsessed Culture, we're not very good at letting people just feel what they're feeling—be sad when they're sad and afraid when they're afraid and so on. In our unhealthy culture we're afraid of big and painful emotions, so it's ingrained in us to quickly try to change them when they happen, even when they are natural and appropriate—like in your case, Yan. Is it okay if I use your situation to make a point? Please let me know if you prefer that I don't."

"No, no, I would love that, Dr. K. I'm okay, really. It felt good to just say it out loud and not have anybody try to make me feel better. That just makes me feel even worse, feeling wrong and like a burden for being sad, you know?"

"Yes, I do know, and that's exactly the point I wanted to make. Do you know why people are always so obsessed with making sad people feel better?"

"Well because nobody wants to be sad, I guess."

"Sure, but when there's a good reason to feel sad—like your situation right now—it can feel almost like an assault when people try to take that feeling away. Am I right?"

"Yes, now that you say it that's kind of what it feels like."

"Deep inside, we need to be able to feel sad," resumed the doctor. "Sadness is our nervous system's way of reacting when we lose something—or even just imagine we might lose something.

"And here's the answer to my own question. When someone near us is sad, it can make us feel sad, too, especially when it's someone we care deeply for. And because our culture has ingrained in us that hard and painful emotions are something that should be avoided, we're not used to being exposed to them. We're used to other people hiding them and doing our best to hide and suppress them ourselves, even though they are a normal part of life. So, because we're not used to being exposed to them, most people feel bad about feeling sad. Yes, here we go again into familiar territory. Sadness is another kind of bodily sensation that makes a lot of people uncomfortable, so they try to avoid or suppress it. So, either consciously or subconsciously, we end up trying to make the other person not be so sad, so that we don't have to feel the sadness this creates in us. We want the discomfort in *ourselves* to go away so we don't have to face it, and when the other person doesn't show their sadness anymore, it does go away. I'm sure you can all relate to this because it happens all the time."

"Wait a minute though, Dr. K," said Elinor. "Are you saying we shouldn't try to comfort people when they're sad? Isn't that a bit harsh?"

"Isn't it just about having true freedom of choice?" Phil added.

"Well, let's ask Yan. Are you okay sharing your feelings and thoughts on this?"

"Sure. When I sense that other people understand what I'm feeling and don't try to change it, that's when I feel their empathy. And then I feel okay that I'm sad. That's what happened right here with your response to my news, Dr. K. But when people try to make me feel better, I feel wrong for being sad. And then I not only feel sad for my situation, but wrong for feeling sad! I feel like I'm a burden to the person I told. So, I actually like being asked about it and talking about it as long as the other person doesn't expect my sadness to go away. I don't know if that makes sense, but that's the way I'm experiencing it."

"Yes, I understand, Yan. Most people have a deep need to feel understood, and the way we've learned to react to each other when we're in situations full of strong and painful emotions makes us feel the exact opposite—it makes us feel wrong. It's hard enough facing the discomfort of sadness, but feeling we are a burden to other people and feeling *wrong* makes it even worse.

"When I saw Yan looking sad, I felt discomfort inside that I identified as sadness in me. And when he told us what had happened, the discomfort increased. Many years ago, my default would have been either not to ask him any more questions or to tell him not to worry too early—just like those other people. But now, I become aware of the tension in myself and am able to stay present with my emotions and tolerate the discomfort they create, the sadness in me. What you all witnessed was me experiencing and staying present with my own feelings and speaking them out loud. That's why I think Yan felt my empathy, because he picked up on my sadness."

"Yes, I really felt you understood, Dr. K. It made me feel embraced, like a big physical hug. I would actually have liked a big physical hug," he said, laughing a little.

"Yes, that's what I thought. I've been on both sides of the situation many times, and that's what I've experienced myself. This is a great example of creating healthy relationships by just being yourself. I was present with what was happening in me while, at the same time, staying present with what was happening outside me—in you, Yan. I expressed what I thought and felt. I was just being myself when I expressed that I was really sorry to hear what happened to you. As usual, this is quite simple. And as usual, it's not necessarily easy."

Dr. Krinksted looked at all the people that he now knew pretty intimately before he continued, "And what makes this possible?"

"I'll answer that, Dr. K," said Melanie. "It's the ability to be aware of and tolerate the discomfort in ourselves when it shows up, not needing it to go away. It's when we have a hard time tolerating the discomfort in ourselves, discomfort that we might not even be aware of, that we don't even have a choice but to try to make the other person feel better. In fact, to make them responsible for making *us* feel better by trying to feel better themselves or hiding it. If we can't tolerate it, as we've learned, we do whatever we need to do to make it go away, no matter if it's irrational or unwise."

It's about creating the situation where we have the most freedom of choice to act wisely.

Dr. Krinksted nodded and gave them a moment to process what Melanie had said. "And Phil," he continued, "you're right in your point about true freedom of choice. It's not about *never or always* having to do something. It's about creating the situation where we have *the most freedom of choice* to act in a way that leads to the outcome we want from our actions. Keeping the ability to act wisely."

Again, the doctor paused, knowing this might still be difficult to grasp for some in the group since it was so different from what had been ingrained in them growing up. "And what you just told us, Yan, is tough shit, I know—and that's how life is sometimes and there's no hiding from that fact. Actually, this leads perfectly into the training I gave you last time we met. I'd like to hear your experiences before I give you more of my thoughts on the subject. Is it okay with you to continue, Yan?"

"Yes, I'm fine with that, please do."

"Okay, who'll start us off?"

"I will, Dr. K," said Diana. "I found what you asked us to do at our last meeting really hard. I realized how often I go on autopilot. It's like I'm not 100 percent there most of the time, if you know what I mean. Of course, I'm there, but moment to moment, I'm definitely much less aware of everything that happens than I could be, and suddenly it's dinnertime or even bedtime, and it's like I don't know where all the hours went. It's almost as if I've been partly sleepwalking. It's scary how I let so much of life just pass by without taking it in."

"I know what you mean, Diana," said Harini. "When Friday comes around, sometimes I wonder where the week went. Of course, I haven't been asleep, but I definitely haven't been fully awake through it all either."

"That's how I used to feel too," said Alex. "It's true that I am very busy, and that hasn't changed, but this feeling of time flying by has changed for me over these past months, even before our last meeting. It's like I started consciously taking in more of what was happening in me and around me more of the time by doing the first exercises, almost as if I was developing an awareness skill—I don't know if there's such a thing, but that's how it felt to me. But I noticed small things much more—like the snow hitting my face as I walked to my car in the morning, how the wind moved the treetops about, and what my morning coffee actually tasted like. I think Barbara wondered what had happened to me!"

"Yes, but I liked it!" said Barbara, laughing. "Seriously, I was quite surprised at first to see you noticing those little things and even mentioning them to me. Actually, I think it helped me become more aware too."

"And when you asked us last time to become aware of as much as possible every moment, even when there's no discomfort in our bodies, I realized that's exactly what had been happening already," Alex added.

"And did you find that you usually weren't aware of much throughout the day?" Dr. Krinksted asked.

"Yes, I think that was my default before, but that definitely started to change some time ago, and the 1 Minute Reminder you gave us two meetings ago pulled me in this direction even more. I pretty much do it every hour these days, and I see it as a kind of alarm clock to switch me off autopilot."

"That's great news, Alex. What about the rest of you?"

"Yes, I did it, but a little differently," said Elinor. "In some situations, I've felt in the past that I was far from fully present, and my mind was kind of wandering, instead of paying attention. This often happens at work in meetings, or even sometimes when I'm supposedly listening to my kids telling me about their day. So, I've used the training to become more fully present in these situations, because to be honest, it's just not within my reach right now to notice what I'm noticing 24/7."

She paused briefly. "And by the way, Dr. K, while I said this out loud right now, I did feel a discomfort in my body, but I did it anyway!"

The doctor laughed. "Well, sounds like a wise way for you to do it, Elinor. And probably a great way to start for a lot of people. Any movement in this direction counts and will decrease the feeling of life flying by too quickly. How has it worked out for you in those situations you mentioned?"

"Well, it was really hard at the beginning. I was glad your training helped me handle the discomfort in my body, because for the first couple of weeks I felt like a total failure. My mind would be wandering all over the place all the time. But that's started to change in the last couple of weeks. I often notice that when the chatter in my mind starts distracting me, I'm more able to listen and stay present to it—do you know what I mean, Dr. K?"

"Yes, I do, Elinor. That's maybe even better than you think, because being fully aware in any given moment includes listening to your thoughts when they start wandering, just as you described. People often get this wrong, thinking it's a matter of stopping the thoughts altogether, stopping the inner dialogue, or not listening to the thoughts. But that's not the way to go. First of all, it's impossible because our thoughts really have a life of their own. They just come and go, so nobody can stop them. And secondly, not listening to them when they are there is the opposite of being fully aware of as much as possible in that moment. If you are ever to get to a point where your head is less filled with thoughts, you must listen to them. Remember, your thoughts are your friends, not your enemy. If you don't listen, you're not able to evaluate what they're trying to tell you, which will typically make them even more persistent. This is part of why we end up with the mind-chatter and overthinking that so many people know all too well. Of course, you've already experienced some of the benefits of being aware of your thoughts, but I wanted to underline it because trying to stop them or ignoring these thoughts is just another example of the bad advice that's so typical in our unhealthy culture."

Everyone nodded, their faces expressing their concentration.

"I do want to point out, though, that listening to your thoughts doesn't mean believing them! Never act as if they're speaking the truth because very often, they're not. But you do have to listen to them in order to make that distinction. They're part of the alarm system in us human beings that is so crucial for our survival. So, trying not to listen to your thoughts altogether is a huge mistake. No, what you have to do is engage your thoughts and your alarms with curiosity and treat tension and anxiety like the friends they really are, which is actually what I'm teaching you to do with this training.

"Elinor, can you tell us what your thoughts, your *alarms* to use this new word, are typically about?"

"Yes, it's always about something I need to remember to do, or how to solve or avoid some problem—or at least what my mind perceives as a problem, to be precise."

"I'm glad you added that last bit, Elinor. I think what you mean is something that your mind thinks will create discomfort if you don't act on it, or something your mind thinks will feel good in your body, so it doesn't want you to miss it, right?"

Listening to your thoughts doesn't mean believing them!

"Yes, and I think that's why it has started changing for me, because being aware of what these thoughts are telling me lets me stay present. Most of the time, it's something that's already on my to-do list or on my calendar, so by listening to the thoughts, I can let them go more easily because I know whatever comes up is being taken care of. Just like you said, Dr. K, it's as if the thoughts keep repeating until they know they've been heard, but they get louder and more and more persistent when they're ignored. Just like when children don't feel seen or heard, they do more to gain their parents' attention. And just like kids, thoughts sometimes act inappropriately—unwisely—if that's the only way they'll get attention."

Elinor smiled. "But this changes when I actually hear my thoughts and listen to them. Saying this out loud—I think it sounds a bit odd, but it's how I experience it."

"Well, that's how I experience it too!" said Dr. Krinksted. "And it's quite fantastic that by simply listening to these voices—which really represent our nervous system's analysis of a given situation—and taking their message into account, they often stop repeating themselves. Which means our mind chatter is reduced."

"I agree," said Cliff. "I've always had a hard time being really present for long periods of time, but this is beginning to change since I started this training."

"You're both making exactly my point," said Dr. Krinksted, smiling. "Thanks! What I consider the ultimate life benefit of this training is what you're describing here, what you call *being more present and aware*: taking in more of what happens inside us and around us while it happens. In my experience, that's what most people are really longing for—and this might be subconsciously."

Laura had a comment, "I think I've read somewhere that on our death bed, what's most important to people is feeling they have lived a full and rich life when looking back."

"That wouldn't surprise me, Laura, if that's true. And all this training of your awareness is exactly what will make this happen."

"Wow!" said Melanie. "That's so exciting!"

Dr. Krinksted smiled. "Yes, it is Melanie. By training this way, you'll be more present with whatever life throws at you and experience a wider range of emotions, both the painful and pleasant ones, instead of trying to get rid of or suppress the hard ones. At the same time, you'll experience *everything* more and more, both the uncomfortable and what feels great."

"So, the sum of *all this* is what will defy this feeling of being on autopilot and time flying by too quickly and give us this deep sense that we're living a full and rich every day instead?" asked Alex. "And that's what you call the ultimate life benefit?"

"Yes, that's right, Alex. All of us here are fortunate to live in parts of the world where mere survival is rarely an issue anymore. So, the problems we feel we have—from small, annoying bad habits, to worry, self-doubt and self-criticism, to less than optimal relationships, to time flying by too quickly—all these spring from the same root cause: our improficiency at and underuse of consciously being aware of as much as possible of what happens in us and around us all the time."

"So, just to be clear one more time, Dr. K," said Diana. "You're not saying we should forget about performing well and doing a good job altogether. All you're saying is that our primary focus should be our awareness and training this ability or skill or whatever we call this, right?"

"Yes, thanks for clearing that up, Diana. As we've discussed before, there's absolutely nothing wrong with trying hard and wanting to do our best. On the contrary, it's a natural thing for us human beings to enjoy exerting ourselves and wanting to do a great job. It's the obsession part that's the villain—the villain that's making so many people, from young to old, feel like they're on autopilot in a rat race and that no matter how much they are or do, it's never enough. And of course, there's nothing wrong with wanting to feel good instead of bad and working your ass off to make that happen.

"The thing that hurts us is *needing* to feel good instead of just *wanting* to feel good. It's the obsession part. It's the needing part that makes us feel inadequate and frustrated. It's the needing part that takes away all your power, letting the more primitive parts of your brain take over, making you act more irrationally, putting you on autopilot, and shifting the power away from a wise and balanced approach. Just wanting or preferring something instead of needing it keeps the connections open to the rational parts of your brain, so that you can make wise decisions—including the option of not doing anything and just tolerating the discomfort. You know the drill by now!"

"Okay," said Alex, "I'm an IT nerd, and I have this metaphor in my head right now that I want to share with you. What you've been describing as being more aware, more present, Doc—it's as if I've been consciously experiencing more bits per second lately instead of living on autopilot and consciously experiencing less bits per second. So, when I take more bits in at any moment, my life doesn't seem to fly by quite so quickly. Right?"

"Well, I've no idea what bits per second are," said Yan. "But it sounds as if it's just your way of saying what we're all experiencing, so I'm good with it, Alex!"

Alex laughed—something he might not have done at the beginning of training.

"That's funny," said Dr. Krinksted. "One of my private clients used the exact same metaphor. She said that before the training it was like she wasn't taking in more than one bit per moment, and after doing all the training, she was now experiencing taking in about twelve bits per moment, which made a year feel like a year instead of a year feeling like a month. That's how she explained that time had slowed down for her in a positive way."

Alex pumped his fist in the air. "Yes! That's exactly what I get too. I'm glad you have other nerds in your life, Dr. K."

"Actually, I really love this metaphor," said Dr. Krinksted. "Just think of all the things we do lifestyle-wise to try to prolong our lives. But by training this simple way, this woman felt her life experience increased by a factor of twelve! Compare that to how a healthy lifestyle might be able to extend our lives by say, ten years, which is only an increase of around a factor of 1.1. Not that we shouldn't do both, of course, but if the factor 1.1 creates all kinds of stress, worry, and autopiloting, so it's at the expense of the factor twelve, it's an unwise trade-off."

"Holy smokes, Dr. K," said Alex. "Who knew you were a fellow nerd?!"

Dr. Krinksted laughed.

"Here's another metaphor," said Laura. "It's like going in the dark with a flashlight. What the flashlight lights up is what I'm conscious of, and everything in the dark is what I don't notice. And what I am training now is two things: I'm increasing the area my flashlight lights up, so that I'm conscious of a bigger area any given moment. And I'm increasing the flashlight's ability to point in different directions, including pointing at areas that are important for me to see even though they make me feel uncomfortable."

"Thanks, Laura, that's another great way to describe it." Dr. Krinksted took a deep breath. "Well, now you all know why I call this the ultimate life benefit. Even though this simple training makes us feel better about ourselves and our lives, it can in no way compare to the benefit of living a life that's fuller and richer in experience, giving us a deeper sense that we're living a full and rich life every day. And you'll get this ultimate benefit without changing even one single thing in your life, solely by increasing your awareness."

The irrepressible Melanie clapped her hands enthusiastically.

"Wow, I'm on a roll again," said Dr. Krinksted, laughing. "It feels so important to me that you are all getting this. Because it has been such a game changer in my own life and in the lives of so many people I've worked with, I don't want anybody else to let any more of their life just fly by. I want everybody to also feel good about themselves and their lives—and to experience a full and rich life, no matter their life circumstances at any given time. We all deserve that, and we can all achieve this if we start training the simple way you've all learned here. My parents died at a young age, and maybe that's where I got this focus in my own life. I know that life is too short and important to be wasted moving on autopilot and not drinking in every last drop of it while we're alive. Even if many days seem to be alike or when life might challenge us, it's still about being present and taking everything in. Being human is not just about feeling happy. It's about feeling everything."

Nobody spoke, and all the faces appeared more serious at Dr. Krinksted's last comment. A little voice in Dr. Krinksted's head told him that it might have been because he mentioned his parents' early deaths. "Sorry, I didn't mean to make you feel uncomfortable—although I know you can handle it," Dr. Krinksted said and smiled.

With that, the smiles came back to their faces.

"Okay, let's meet one last time in a few months. I won't give you any new focus for your training. Just keep using what you've learned in whatever way it feels right for you. Sound good?"

Everyone nodded.

Then Irene spoke up, "Yan, I hope the very best for you and your family. I'll send you and your daughter some good energy."

"Yes," said Dr. Krinksted, "thanks for expressing that, Irene."

"Thank you all so much for listening to me today. It meant a lot to me. In fact, at this point, you all mean a lot to me," Yan replied.

Although the last comments made the energy in the room go down a little, the overall feeling in the group was one of presence and intimacy. Dr. Krinksted felt happy that it seemed like everybody was steadily moving towards being more aware in their lives.

CHAPTER 11

The Ultimate Life Skill

The Last Meeting

Conscious that he was nearing the end of his time with this group of people, Dr. Krinksted felt a little sad. Nonetheless, he looked forward to this last session as the screens lit up one by one.

"Hello everybody!" he said to lots of smiling replies.

Before he had a chance to say more, Irene spoke up. "Hi Dr. K," she said. "I hope you don't mind me jumping in like this, but I really want to know how Yan's daughter is doing. I've been thinking about her a lot."

"Yes, I would like to know that too," said the doctor. "Yan, will you give us an update?"

Everyone could see from his expression that Yan was feeling much better than last time, and he confirmed that the news was good. "She has had surgery and chemotherapy, which is now over. It wasn't easy for her, but it went well. Thank you so much for asking—I felt your support surrounding me when we spoke last time."

After a few more supporting comments for Yan, Dr. Krinksted resumed in the usual way. "Well, it's been almost twelve months, and we're reaching the end of our training. I can't wait to hear all your experiences since we last met. Who'll start us off?"

Yan spoke again. "Well, I have something to report. As you can imagine, when we first learned of Marie's illness, we were filled with emotions—and not the kind any of us want. We were scared, we were angry, we were desperately worried. What I want to share is the role of this training in getting me through this horrible time. In spite of what was ingrained in me, I reminded myself that all these emotions were natural given the terrible circumstances. I did a lot of sitting with all the tension, emotions, and thoughts I had. Of course, this didn't make them go away, but I was somehow better able to live with it all without losing my ability to act wisely. And what makes me happy about all that is that even though my wife and daughter haven't done this training, my new approach to life seemed to help them too. They've both expressed an interest in learning more once this course is over, so I expect to start helping them with it soon."

"Yan," said Dr. Krinksted, "knowing that what I teach has helped you go through one of life's most difficult situations makes me grateful."

"Yes," said Melanie. "That's awesome, Yan!"

"Good for you, Yan," said Phil.

"Yes, I'm happy for you and your family, Yan," said Hannah in her quiet way.

"Virtual high-five to you, Yan!" said Rohan, holding his palm up to the screen and receiving an answering gesture from a smiling Yan.

"All right, who else has something to tell us?" Dr. Krinksted asked.

"Well," said Elinor, "I know I've said this before, but I can't tell you how happy I am that we got stuck on that island! I simply can't imagine living my life the way I used to. What has happened in my life is pretty miraculous—I know you wouldn't call it that, Dr. K, but that's how it feels to me. And it's not just about my own inner experience anymore. People close to me are noticing that I act differently, and they're starting to ask questions about it."

"I can tell you that's true," added Phil. "Naturally, I see the differences in Elinor, and because I'm in the training, too, I understand the reasons, but I've heard our friends mention it to her also."

The doctor smiled. "That's interesting. What are your friends noticing, Elinor?"

"The most common thing I've heard is that I seem more balanced and present. And I now understand that balanced doesn't mean always being in the middle, but being able to wisely stretch in different directions and return to the middle without falling.

"My best friend Joan mentioned that it seems to her I've started to express my opinions and show my true self more. It appears my friendships are becoming more intimate, even with Joan, who I felt was really close before I started all this training. I sense maybe some of them miss the old me, you know, the Elinor who was always trying to please!" Elinor laughed. "But at the same time, they're interested in learning how I came to be this way and maybe willing to try to make some changes for themselves."

"That's good news. And what about what you call your own inner experience?"

"Well, at the beginning, I was using your 3/3 Routine to expose and confront the discomfort in my body, and it definitely made me less dependent on my retail habit!"

"Yes, and I'm happy about that too," said Phil with a laugh.

"But the more I do the 3/3 Routine, the less it seems like a tool and the more it becomes who I am—a wise person who listens to herself as well as others and shows up more present and grounded, making more conscious decisions more often. Of course, there are still times when I have to remind myself to be aware of what's going on in my body and mind as well as outside of me, instead of running on autopilot. But in general, it's happening more by itself. It's no exaggeration to say it has changed my life."

She turned to her husband and said, "I also want Phil to speak up here, and I'm mentioning it just in case he doesn't. Phil, why don't you stand up and let everyone see the new, slimmed-down version of you?"

As everyone smiled and applauded, Phil did just that. He blushed a bit and said, "Yes, you might remember what a terrible eater I was. When I started using your 3/3 to work on that, the weight started slowly coming off. Any time I've tried typical diets before, I was always checking the scale every morning, but not this time. To be honest, I don't even know how much weight I've lost or what I weigh now. I just know I feel a lot better. It's a fantastic feeling being more in control, and I'm absolutely sure I'll never go back to my old ways! So, all this has been a real life changer for both Elinor and me—and for our relationship too, right honey?"

"Absolutely!" replied a smiling Elinor.

"That's great," said Rohan. "I'm really pleased for you both. Something interesting—and quite marvelous—has happened for me too. I think I was always chasing happy feelings in some way or another. It's pretty obvious to me now how all my flirting was about the happy feelings that arose in me when I felt a woman liked me, even though I wasn't even aware of it at the time. But that frantic craving for happy feelings seems to have stopped. I don't really understand why, but it seems that when I experience everything more, it makes my life better and even easier. Now, I can handle more intense emotions of all kinds, so I don't have the same need to suppress them with happy feelings. Don't get me wrong, I'd rather be happy most of the time, but I get that life will feel hard sometimes, no matter what, and that unhappy feelings are part of any normal life."

"I'm glad you've reached this point, Rohan," said Dr. Krinksted, "as it means you have overcome those old ideas that are ingrained in us—you know, expecting of ourselves that we should always be superhumans who live perfect lives and, therefore, always try to avoid or suppress the so-called bad emotions. As I've said repeatedly, and I'll say it again: What most people really yearn for is experiencing a full and rich life every day, which is more about experiencing *everything*—including the hardships that all human lives contain—than only experiencing happy feelings. If this wasn't true, we could all become junkies because that's what hard drugs do, create ecstatic feelings. But deep down we know that a life with only happy feelings would not be as fulfilling as one in which we experience the ups and downs of a normal life. There's so much quality in the contrasts: Without night we wouldn't appreciate day. Without rainy days we wouldn't enjoy the sun as much. Without loss, we wouldn't be as grateful for all the love we have in our lives.

Experiencing a full and rich life every day is about experiencing everything— including the hardships.

"In many ways, we can compare living to reading a book. Nobody wants to read a novel with no challenges, obstacles, or hardships. A book with only happy people and situations would be boring! But we often forget that fact in those moments when we're experiencing hard and unpleasant emotions, and we forget that the hard stuff is part of the contrast necessary for us to experience living the most full and rich life."

"Yes," said Rohan, "but you said that all this can't be blamed on our unhealthy culture alone, that it's also because of our normal human nature, right? Can you say more about that again, please?"

"Right. We've touched upon this many times before. It's a normal part of human nature to always yearn for something better or different than we have, to do better and have more. Of course, we want to do what makes us feel good, and there's nothing wrong with that. The problem arises when we believe that there's something wrong when we're not happy, and we do anything and everything to prevent it from happening or to numb or suppress it when it happens. The fact is that life *is* hard; it's not easy to be a human being. So, when it's ingrained in us that when we are not feeling happy there's something wrong with us or our lives, we'll end up in this constant battle to create something that's impossible to achieve. Can you see how this leads to so many of the challenges we all face in our modern, hectic world? Stress, dysfunctional relationships, feelings of inadequacy, and low self-worth—you name it."

"That's the ultimate benefit of this training, to experience all of life more fully, the good as well as the ugly."

Knowing he had said all this before and understanding that it was important for them to absorb it, the doctor paused, looking at all the faces and smiling.

Diana raised her hand. "Here's probably the best thing I've experienced during our time together. Before, I had this need to constantly try to make things happen, to take vacations and have other experiences to make my life interesting and exciting. But that need has changed quite a lot. It's not that I don't want variety in my life or enjoy vacations, but I don't crave these things anymore. I think it's because I'm more present and experience all the things that are happening in my normal life. Now that I'm taking more in, I'm experiencing such a variety of thoughts and feelings all the time, even though any two days might look pretty much the same from the outside. This makes my life seem much fuller and richer now, just like you've talked about, Dr. K. I must say I don't envy people who are fighting the almost constant battle to make their outside circumstances be a certain perfect way to avoid discomfort they can't tolerate, now that I no longer do. Having been there myself makes it hard to witness in other people, especially people I care about. I'd like to inspire some of them to make the changes I have—maybe by getting them to read your book or doing your online course when you've created it," she said with a wink at Dr. Krinksted. "But of course, even though it makes me sad, I have a real of choice as to whether or not to do anything about it, so I can act wisely around this."

"So how *do* you handle it?" asked Jill.

"Sometimes I just notice the sadness and frustration I'm experiencing," said Diana, "and I don't do anything. After all, I don't want to lecture people. And I've come to enjoy this way of living, just listening to my own thoughts and urges and doing what feels right in the moment, taking as much as possible into account. Sometimes, I say something even though it might create some tension—I really don't struggle much with it. I guess I pretty much play it by ear, simply being who I am. Kind of what Dr. K told us earlier about going for effortless.

"We're all different, and I don't presume to know what's best for anybody else. But if I could help others break free from the cultural conditioning that makes them feel bad about themselves and the life they live and makes time seem to fly by way too quickly for them, then I'd love to do that.

"But all in all, I think it's best just to be an example, a role model if you'd like, rather than try to force the ideas on anyone else. I know if somebody had tried to tell me twelve months ago that I was wasting my life living too much on autopilot, it would have put me on the defensive, and I wouldn't have listened."

"So," said Dr. Krinksted, "having created a situation in yourself where you're better able to make a wise and conscious decision on how to handle this wisely is not only good for you but also for the people around you?"

"Exactly."

"Who else has something for us?"

Irene leaned a little towards her camera and spoke, "I love all the benefits, Dr. K," she said. "Even the smaller ones, like being more in control of my little bad habits. But the biggest change for me is in my relationships. Both in my relationship with myself and with the people I hold dear. I still love being there for people and generally being generous, but I know I'm not trying to please everyone all the time the way I used to. I see now that I needed to make everybody else happy in order to feel good about myself. It's such a relief to take my own wants and needs into account as well as others. I truly understand the idea of healthy selfishness—that *also me* does not mean *only me*.

"I can say this here because I've already discussed it with them, but both Cliff and Melanie have told me they feel relieved because they don't always feel they have to work hard to make sure I'm not disappointed in them. It's true that I used to be a bit of a martyr, wanting people to recognize all I was doing for them. But taking responsibility for my own needs and being able to say no when it's the wise thing to do has changed all that."

Melanie silently put her hands together to show a heart, and Irene blew her a kiss back.

Jill took over. "For me, it's all about being present in my life. As you all know, my two daughters were a source of great frustration. All their bickering and the constant arguing got on my nerves. Of course, I thought at the time they were the ones who needed to change, but as it turns out, the changes in me are what makes the difference in all our lives."

"That's very interesting, Jill," said Dr. Krinksted.

"Yes, I've noticed that when I'm truly present with my kids, listening not only to what they say but also to what seems to be happening in them—kind of the way I'm now aware of what's happening in myself— they don't fight and argue with each other as much. I can see now that a lot of their behavior before was probably an effort to get my attention because even though I was with them, I was often doing or thinking about something else at the same time. It was as if I was there without really being there. I wasn't truly present. Do you know what I mean?"

"Yes, I'm reminded of a proverb I've heard," said the doctor. "I'm translating it from Danish, so I hope you still get the meaning. It says: *Togetherness without presence is like going to a restaurant and having the menu instead of the meal—it leaves you twice as hungry.*

"That really speaks to me because real presence is so absent in our hectic modern world. Everybody misses it, even though most are not even aware of what they're missing. Real presence starts with experiencing fully what's happening in our own bodies and minds. I think we'd all agree it's much nicer to be with people who are truly present. I know I hate it when I'm talking to somebody, and I sense that they're not really there. It makes me feel unimportant when they are not really listening."

"Oh, can I relate to that!" said Phil.

"No kidding," said Melanie.

"Can I ask a question?" asked Laura.

"Of course," said the doctor.

"I have a friend who had cancer when she was a teenager and was cured. I've realized that a lot of what we're experiencing and talking about I've seen in her for years. So, I'm wondering if a near-death experience like that somehow makes you naturally better at all this—being present and automatically being able to choose more consciously and wisely when to say yes and when to say no. She does seem to savor every moment of her life more than most people do, good as well as bad, which I guess is another way of saying experiencing as much as possible every moment. It's like she effortlessly gets the last drop of each day she's alive without being stressed about it. Does it make sense that this is what happens when we're confronted with the fact that life could suddenly be over sooner than later like she was?"

"Yes," said Dr. Krinksted, "I think you're right about that, Laura. When confronted with our own mortality through a near-death experience it becomes obvious how each moment is precious, no matter if we're feeling great or challenged. It makes you instantly realize that life is simply too short to be wasted letting time just fly by while living on auto-pilot and not experiencing as much as possible every single moment. Also, a near-death experience typically makes a person see things more for what they really are, like we've been talking about, enabling them to act more wisely.

"Since it's not possible to fabricate a near-death experience, it would be nice to achieve some of the same realization in another way. And I have found that training your awareness the way I am teaching will do just that. It's not the only way, but I've found it to be the most direct and quickest way."

Life is simply too short to be wasted letting time just fly by while living on auto-pilot.

"I'm curious, Dr. K," said Cliff. "You told us the title of your book is The Ultimate Life Skill, but you haven't mentioned this skill at all throughout all our time together? We're coming to an end, so what is this ultimate life skill, and why haven't you even mentioned it to us?"

Dr. Krinksted paused for a second before speaking, "Thank you for this question, Cliff, because I think we're now ready for this last bit I would like to tell you guys before we can finish our time together. It's time for me to tell you what *The Ultimate Life Skill* is."

Dr. Krinksted smiled. "I'll start with the short version: All the training you've done from the very start of our time together has increased your proficiency in one particular skill—and it's the skill I have come to call *The Ultimate Life Skill."*

Everybody looked a little confused.

Dr. Krinksted continued, "The only thing you've basically been training toward in all our assignments is your ability to be aware. Your awareness. And it's actually both your ability and use of this awareness ability. Being aware of as much as possible while it happens instead of not being aware while it happens—instead of being on autopilot as we've called it."

People still looked puzzled as Dr. Krinksted continued, "And the technical word for awareness, for being aware of something while it happens, is consciousness. Actually, if we break the word consciousness into its parts, that's exactly what it means. *Con* meaning *with* and *scious* meaning *knowledge."*

"Wait a minute, Dr. K," said Alex, sounding a bit like his old confrontational self. "Are you saying that what we've really been training all along is what consciousness means?"

Dr. Krinksted smiled again. "Yes, that's right, Alex. Training your ability to be and stay aware of what happens in your body and mind while it happens—it's all the same as training your ability to be and stay conscious. Depending on how we view consciousness, what is happening in your bodies and minds are all we can be conscious of. The thing is, we experience what happens outside ourselves through our senses and how our brains process events. And this happens inside our bodies and minds. At the start, we amplified what we were looking for to make it easier for you to become conscious of it, creating tension and uncomfortable sensations by postponing the act of giving in to a bad habit. And then, step by step, you improved your proficiency at being conscious of what is happening in your body and mind in other more difficult situations.

"But this is unnecessarily technical again, so there's no need to try to understand this in depth. The bottom line is that consciousness is just your ability to notice the three things we can in any given moment: what happens in our bodies, what happens in our minds, and what happens outside ourselves. And for all practical purposes, noticing, awareness, consciousness, and listening to ourselves are just different ways of expressing the same thing."

"Why didn't you just call it consciousness from the start?" asked Alex.

"Because in my experience, people tune out when they hear the word consciousness. It's probably because it seems too abstract and difficult to understand. But it's really not that hard when you have experienced it again and again as you have. That's why I wait to explain it until someone has had their own experience of it."

"But why do you call this The Ultimate Life Skill?" Laura realized Dr. Krinksted hadn't answered all Cliff's questions.

"Well, there are so many reasons for this I don't know where to start. But let me try. Early in the process, I realized that this skill is the single most important life skill for us human beings. If you practice this skill on a daily basis, you really don't need to practice anything else. When you train in this skill while there's tension in your body, you'll automatically start tolerating the tension better, letting you keep more access to the reasoning parts of your brain. This creates the situation where you have the most freedom of choice to act in a wise, healthy, and balanced way, being hijacked less often by the more primitive part of your brain. This is a big part of the reason you're feeling better about yourself and the life you live now, right?"

Dr. Krinksted did not expect an answer and continued, "Your proficiency and use of this skill stops life from flying by too fast, making you experience a more full, rich life of everything that life offers—what feels amazing as well as what feels hard and painful."

The doctor took a deep breath. "And, on top of these benefits for yourself, always having a part of your focus on what is happening in your body and mind while it happens, and being able to tolerate whatever happens inside your own skin, *The Ultimate Life Skill* makes you part of the solution instead of part of the problem in our unhealthy culture.

"There's really nothing new in what I'm saying here; it's everything we've talked about and you've experienced for yourself the last twelve months that I'm repeating for you."

All the faces on the screens were totally concentrating on Dr. Krinksted's words, knowing that what he was saying now was the crux of the whole thing.

"But here's what is new that adds to the reasons I call consciousness *The Ultimate Life Skill.* Adding to everything I just said, our consciousness is also the human skill that separates us most from all other creatures on the planet. Our consciousness is what has made us rulers of the planet—for better and for worse. So it's not just a word for me. For all these different reasons, I truly see it as *The Ultimate Life Skill.*"

Dr. Krinksted looked around the group. When he noticed that nobody seemed to have any comments or burning questions, he continued, "Also, think about this. If you could live forever and have whatever in your life you could dream of, but you had to trade it for your consciousness so that you wouldn't be able to experience any of it consciously, would you say yes? Or would you rather have a real life with all its ups and downs but experience it fully?"

Although it was a rhetorical question, Dr. Krinksted was glad to see all the heads nodding once again.

Then Phil spoke up. "I know a woman who had a stroke, and now she can never remember what happened just a few minutes ago. Almost nothing is stored in her brain anymore. The weird thing is that she's almost always happy—maybe because she doesn't remember all the bad things. It's kind of the situation you just described, Dr. K, because even though she's happy and smiling when I see her, I don't think anyone would like to be in her shoes. I know I wouldn't. And I know her family is devastated."

Dr. Krinksted allowed a silence to follow because he could see from their expressions that they were processing all this information.

Finally, Rohan spoke, "You know, Dr. K, I think all this is giving me an answer to a question I've had for a long time. An uncle of mine died by suicide after being diagnosed with an odd kind of dementia. He just couldn't stand the idea of ending up being a burden to other people. I could totally understand that, and in fact, I wondered why more people don't take their own lives given all the suffering there is in the world, even in the rich and privileged parts. But maybe what we're talking about is the answer. Experiencing life is so much more important than anything. Almost no matter how much we might be suffering, we'd somehow rather keep experiencing it than stop our experience altogether by ending our life."

Melanie took over. "Yes, because experiencing is actually what happens when using The Ultimate Life Skill—our consciousness, isn't it? No consciousness—no experience, right?" Melanie looked at all the faces. "Experience is the reason it's so hard to explain all this to people who haven't been through the training we've had together. When I've tried to tell people about it, they end up with a glazed look in their eyes as if I was speaking a foreign language! I can't seem to describe it in a way they understand."

"I know what you mean, Melanie," said Elinor. "And it's quite sad, because after getting so much out of it myself, I want everybody else to get the same benefits. I can't imagine never having come across this. It's as if I'm a different person inside now, even though my life looks pretty much the same from the outside. All this comes from the simple ability to always have some awareness of what's happening in my body and mind as it occurs from moment to moment. Now I'm more conscious, more of the time, and less on autopilot where time seems to fly by too quickly. I completely understand why you call this The Ultimate Life Skill, Dr. K!"

"Yes," said Diana, picking up when Elinor stopped. "Just like Rohan, I've started to notice that now, when I experience everything more fully, happiness isn't an issue anymore. I haven't even purposely tried to make life seem nicer; I simply experience all the contrasts that make life full and rich. I can see how I made my life less interesting and exciting because I was trying so hard to avoid, numb, or hide the more hard and painful situations and feelings that life could throw at me. Instead of also savoring these parts of life by being max conscious of it all when it happens. I can even feel self-pity and accept this now. Wow! What a relief just admitting this to you guys—actually accepting that I'm sometimes weak, that I'm not superhuman. Why is it that we're better at letting other people *just be human* but demand that we be superhuman ourselves?"

"Sorry, Diana," said Jill, "but I don't agree with you on that last point. I think we keep each other prisoner when we don't show ourselves authentically, when we don't have the courage to show our own so-called weaknesses. We indirectly teach everybody around us, especially those we love the most, that those parts are not okay, that they should be avoided or suppressed like we're ingrained to do. I think it's our actions that mean the most—if we show by example what it means to be human, show that the beliefs in our Performance and Perfection Obsessed Culture are wrong, we might have a better chance of helping other people do it too."

Jill continued, "Going back to what Diana just said about how her focus on happiness evaporated, I experienced the same thing. After learning to be more consistently present each moment—being more conscious, as you now call it—I also feel that happiness isn't an issue anymore. I think in today's society, we've got the idea of happiness all wrong; we've distorted it. Most people think happiness means that everything has to be good, and we always have to feel good, and when we don't, something must be wrong. So, we really can't be happy by that definition, which is why I think the notion of happiness causes stress for so many people. It's just not attainable as a life situation that must be there all the time."

Being human is not about feeling happy all the time. It's about experiencing everything all the time.

"I agree, Jill," said Dr. Krinksted. "Happiness is a feeling rather than a situation. It comes and goes. When happiness is your goal, you're doomed to lose. Of course, it's nice to be happy. But if we believe that's how we should experience life all the time, we're doomed to end up feeling inadequate and unfulfilled because not only won't we feel happy all the time, but we'll feel guilty and inadequate, and, therefore, unhappy about not feeling happy! It goes hand-in-hand with the belief in our culture that if you believe you can do something, you can—so if you can't make it happen, you feel there's something wrong with you. It all leads to unnecessary feelings of inadequacy and frustration. Here's what's true: Being human is not about feeling happy all the time. It's about experiencing everything all the time. And that's *The Ultimate Life Skill*."

Conversation slowly abated as they all realized their time together was coming to an end.

"Well," said Dr. Krinksted, "I'm glad we've had such a good discussion today, as our time together is winding down."

"Can I just interrupt for a moment, Dr. K?" asked Elinor.

"Of course!"

"Well, I would like to be part of the movement away from our Performance and Perfection Obsessed Culture and all the societal pressure that follows. I would love for my friends to know about it and be able to break away from it as I've started to do myself. Yes, actually as many people as possible! And I bet I'm not the only one." Elinor saw a lot of nodding faces and continued, "But I find it hard to explain all this to other people. I was wondering if we couldn't work together on coming up with an approach we could use for that."

"I love that idea, Elinor," said Dr. Krinksted. "I would love if what I teach could start a movement so more people in our culture could feel better about themselves, be more fulfilled, and experience the most full and rich life under their given circumstances. Does anyone have any thoughts on how we could do that?"

"Well, it seems to me the obvious thing is to recommend your book and your online course when it's been created, Dr. K," said Rohan.

The doctor smiled.

"I agree," said Diana. "I will certainly recommend the book and your online course, but how do you suggest we describe what they'll get out of it in a way so that it will be understood?"

There was silence for a few moments as they all thought about this. A few people even started writing on their computers. Dr. Krinksted didn't want to interrupt, as he thought it would be wise to let the ideas come from these people who had just experienced this for themselves.

After a few moments, Laura spoke up and read something from her screen: "From reading Dr. Krinksted's book and taking his online course, I realized that without even being aware of it, our Performance and Perfection Obsessed Culture often makes me act unwisely and leaves me feeling inadequate and unfulfilled. If you read his book or take his online course, Dr. Krinksted will help you see where and how our unhealthy culture affects you and your life negatively. And you'll learn how to break free from it, so you will stop feeling like you are in a rat race in which no matter how much you are or do, it's never enough, while time just seems to fly by too quickly. Instead, you'll be able to wisely prioritize and follow through on what's most important in life and be more pleased with yourself, ultimately experiencing a full and rich life every day.

"I can highly recommend Dr. Krinksted's book and online course because I believe we all deserve to feel good about who we are and the lives we live, even when things are not perfect. I think it's plain wrong that the very culture we live in damages—instead of building up—our ability to feel fulfilled. Also, I'd be happy to chat with you about all this if you like. How about that?"

Several people nodded. It seemed like Laura's wording resonated well with the rest of this group. Laura said she would send a copy to everyone.

Dr. Krinksted took over again. "I feel really sad that this meeting is soon over," he said. "I will miss you all and our recurring conversations a lot. But I also feel happy for the time we've had together and having witnessed how training *The Ultimate Life Skill*—your consciousness—has made positive changes in each of your lives. I want to thank all of you so much for what you've done for me, for my work, and for each other. Please feel free to contact me if you feel like it and know that you can always find me and more information at www.TheUltimateLifeSkill.com. Also, I know you all have each other's email addresses, so you can reach out to each other if you feel like it. Dr. Krinksted hesitated and looked at all the faces on his screen.

Finally he spoke his final words to these fine human beings, "Bye, bye, everybody! Take care!"

"Bye, Dr. K, thanks!"

"Yes, thanks, everybody!"

"Be well, everyone!"

One by one, the screens went dark as everybody said goodbye. Dr. Krinksted allowed himself to feel happy and sad at the same time.

EPILOGUE

So, you've come to the end of the story about the stranded vacationers and *The Ultimate Life Skill.*

As you have discovered in the last couple of chapters, the 3 Minute/3 Step Routine and the 1 Minute Reminder are simple ways to train and automatically start integrating more consciousness into your life, no matter how hectic it might be.

Maybe you've done the 3 Minute/3 Step Routine and the 1 Minute Reminder along the way—or maybe you haven't.

Either way, I hope you now understand how the combination of a normal human nervous system and the obsession with performance and perfection that our culture ingrains in us ruins your ability to be truly fulfilled. By now, you should know that being just human is not just fine, it's normal. Being just human, making mistakes again and again—doing something that definitely doesn't seem great even when you know you have the best intention to do something that serves yourself and the people you love—is what we all have in common.

Hopefully, this has made you feel just a little better about yourself and your life and made you more present and aware, experiencing more of everything—what feels good as well as what feels bad—leaving you with a deeper sense of living a full and rich life every day.

As you know from reading this book, I truly believe that increasing your proficiency to live a more conscious life is the single most important thing you can do if you ever want to be truly fulfilled in life. And to increase your proficiency to live a more conscious life, you need to practice this one way or the other. Training with the 3 Minute/3 Step Routine and the 1 Minute Reminder are the easiest ways I have found to start doing this. If you haven't done these along the way, I invite you to make it a point to start and keep practicing them for the rest of your life in some shape or form.

If you feel like accepting this invitation, I suggest you create a reminder on your phone right now that notifies you once a week to remind you that increasing your consciousness is a task you want to focus on.

You can make the period between notifications longer when you feel you don't need to be reminded as often. You may move towards a month instead of a week, then three months, six months, and finally, just every year, where I suggest you keep it forever.

And every time you see or hear the reminder, stop and notice how you feel about coming back to increasing your awareness by putting the 3/3 Routine and 1 Minute Reminder to work in your life or any other way to increase your level of consciousness that might work better for you.

If this feels and sounds right for you, I suggest you do it now while it's in the front of your mind. That would be the *wise* thing to do—in my opinion.

Please visit our website, www.TheUltimateLifeSkill.com, and consider signing up for our newsletter. This connection will enable us to convey new ways of integrating consciousness into your life that might work even better for you. Also, this could be a way for you to join the growing number of people fighting the Performance and Perfection Obsessed Culture we live in for the benefit of yourself and everybody else. This shift toward more conscious awareness in the world is most important for our kids and the generations to come, so they don't become ingrained with this toxic culture and have to live through all the downsides as you and I have.

And if you don't feel like doing any of this or never get to do any of this, don't worry about it. Remember, it's okay to be just human. You don't need to be superhuman; none of us are.

Thanks for reading my book.
Dr. Peter Kristiansen

Before You Go. . .
If this book added value to your life
and you believe others might benefit from reading it too
please help it reach more people by leaving a review on your
favorite online book retailer.
Thank you!

ACKNOWLEDGMENTS

To my wife for wanting to share our life experience together and for standing by me for good and for worse for almost four decades now—including during all my struggles creating this book.

To my three kids for giving me the amazing life experiences that kids give you.

To all my friends and acquaintances who have listened to all my thoughts about life for so many years.

To my clients who made me have to, and want to, keep refining how I convey this essential knowledge.

To the people who read my early manuscripts and those who gave me feedback along the way.

To my publisher for helping me get my book out to you guys, the readers.

And finally, to life itself, which forced me to create the clarity I needed to feel truly fulfilled myself that consequentially enabled me to write this book for you.

CONTACT THE AUTHOR

If you have any questions, comments, or suggestions as to how this book could be improved, I'd love to hear from you.

If you'd like assistance in being more conscious in your life and acting more wisely, please find my contact information on: www.TheUltimateLifeSkill.com

CONTACT THE AUTHOR

ABOUT THE AUTHOR

Born and raised in Denmark, Dr. Peter Kristiansen's passion and interest have always been on more than how to make people get rid of a disease.

Early in his career, he supplemented his Doctor of Chiropractic degree with studies in the areas of personal and organizational development and leadership, and he exchanged working with patients for working with companies and employees. At the same time, he started offering personal advice to private clients, supplementing traditional life and executive coaching with more direct advice, which gave his clients better and faster results.

Based on his scientific education, his own life challenges and experiences, and his work as a personal advisor, Dr. Kristiansen picked up a significant pattern. He realized that there's one life skill that—second to none—determines how good we feel about ourselves, our lives, and ultimately, how fulfilled we are.

After this realization, he struggled for many years with how he could convey this important fact to a wider audience in a book. He searched for a way that not only taught people this important fact but made the knowledge come into play and give results immediately in peoples' lives while reading.

The Ultimate Life Skill is the end result of this journey.